TRIPLE TESTED • FOR YOUR SUCCESS EVERY TIME

For more than 50 years, *The Australian Women's Weekly* Test Kitchen has been creating marvellous recipes that come with a guarantee of success. First, the recipes always work – just follow the instructions and you too will get the results you see in the photographs. Second, and perhaps more importantly, they are delicious – created by experienced home economists and chefs, all triple-tested and, thanks to their straightforward instructions, easy to make.

LOW-FAT MEALS IN MINUTES

When speed is of the essence – and isn't that almost always these days – it can be tempting to sacrifice sensible nutrition because you're in a hurry. But with *Low-Fat Meals in Minutes*, the creative Test Kitchen team has put together a collection of quick and easy recipes that not only taste delicious, they're good for you, too. So don't think takeaway, think home-cooked instead, and see just how good fast food can be.

Pamela Clark

FOOD EDITOR

Apple and cinnamon cakes with lemon syrup, page 96

Teriyaki beef skewers, page 65

Tomato and borlotti bean soup, page 9

contents

Tuna with char-grilled vegetables, page 35

Eggplant, spinach and butter lettuce salad, page 79

British and North American readers:
Please note that Australian cup and spoon measurements
are metric. A quick conversion guide appears on page 119.

Fast and light – the basics

A low-fat diet does not mean a no-fat diet! Indeed, eating a certain amount of fat is absolutely essential for maintaining good health, energy, and glowing skin and hair. However, most of us eat far more fat than we actually *need* and eating less fat, and less saturated fat in particular, is one of the best things you can do for your health – even if you are not overweight.

The National Heart Foundation recommends that no more than 25 to 30 per cent of your total daily kilojoules should come from fat, which means about 65g of fat per day for men and 50g for women – and as little as possible of these amounts should be saturated fat (the type found in full cream dairy products, animal fats, coconut, palm oil and chocolate).

How can you eat less fat?

Avoid takeaway food, as well as commercial cakes and biscuits. Eat smaller portions of lean meat and increase your consumption of fish, including canned fish. Always remove the skin from chicken and replace high-fat dairy products with low-fat alternatives. Choose olive or canola oil for cooking (and use it sparingly), and remember that fruit, vegetables, breads and cereals should form the major part of your diet.

But reducing the fat in your diet does *not* mean reducing the flavour. Nor does it mean spending hours in the kitchen concocting special diet food. Our simple tips on these pages – and the fabulous recipes to follow – will help make all your meals healthier and lower in fat, even when you're in a hurry.

Be prepared

A well-stocked pantry, refrigerator and freezer guarantee you will always have the necessary ingredients on hand to put together a healthy, interesting meal without too much effort – and relieve the temptation to resort to high-fat, high-cost takeaway.

• Garlic, ginger, chilli, fresh and dried herbs, mustard, chutney, lemon juice, soy and teriyaki sauce, Worcestershire sauce, flavoured vinegars, oyster sauce, pepper or seasoning mixtures are all essential stand-bys for low-fat flavour hits.

Fresh herbs give food a flavour hit.

Essential equipment

A few basic tools make light work of cooking without added fat.

• Heavy-base, non-stick pans, woks and baking dishes make low-fat cooking easy and cleaning effortless.

• Bamboo or stainless-steel steamers, and the microwave oven, produce great results without added fat, especially with fish and vegetables.

• A cast-iron, ridged griddle pan or a barbecue impart a smoky, grilled flavour and create mouth-watering visual appeal – all with a minimum of added fat.

• Baking paper can be used in a variety of ways to eliminate the need for added fat – try lining baking dishes, oven trays and cake pans, making oiling them unnecessary.

• Cooking-oil spray is a boon when you are trying to reduce added fat – a light spray is all that's needed to prevent food from sticking.

Cooking the low-fat way

• Always *measure* the amount of oil you add to a pan, rather than simply adding a slurp by guesswork.

• Don't even *think* of deep-frying! Instead, roast food in a hot oven on a baking-paper-lined oven tray or, if appropriate, steam or microwave food first then crisp in a hot oven after coating lightly with cooking-oil spray. This method produces delicious "baked" potatoes and root vegetables.

• Stir-fry in a wok or non-stick pan rather than shallow-fry.

• Heat your pan or grill before adding oil – it will spread further, so you will need to use less.

• Add the same amount of stock, water, juice, flavoured vinegar or wine to pan as an alternative to oil or butter.

• Roast meat on a rack in a baking dish to allow excess fat to drain away from the meat.

• When slow cooking or stewing, trim all fat from meat and poultry before cooking.

• Prepare casseroles and soups a day ahead and refrigerate so that any fat solidifies on the surface. Skim off all fat before reheating.

• Thicken sauces with pureed vegetables – keep small amounts frozen for the purpose.

Low-fat alternatives

Don't completely deprive yourself – just replace high-fat foods with an appropriate low-fat alternative.

• Instead of ice-cream or cream, try whipped chilled evaporated milk (serve immediately) or whipped low-fat ricotta cheese, flavoured with icing sugar.

Whipped low-fat ricotta.

• Use buttermilk or low-fat yogurt in place of sour cream and full-fat yogurt.

• Use fillo pastry as an alternative to shortcrust or puff pastry. Coat fillo sheets lightly with cooking-oil spray or water, better yet, between layers.

• Instead of oil, use the same amount of stock or water. For salad dressings, use an oil-free variety.

Make salad dressings without oil.

- Make your own reduced-fat version of coconut cream by soaking desiccated coconut in low-fat milk; stand for 30 minutes, then strain over a bowl and discard coconut. You can also add a few drops of coconut essence to evaporated low-fat skim milk.

- Substitute low-fat margarine or light cream cheese for butter and margarine.

- Always choose a low-fat variety of commercial mayonnaise.

- When selecting cheese, choose low-fat cheddar, mozzarella, bocconcini and ricotta varieties, and remember that a small amount of parmesan cheese (although full-fat) actually gives twice as much flavour as many other cheeses, so you can use less.

- When appropriate, double the cooking quantities and freeze half of the dish for another time.

- Cutting meat or poultry into individual portions, strips or cubes before freezing will save time in meal preparation. Make the package as flat as possible so it will defrost quickly when needed.

Microwave shortcuts

Learn to love your microwave oven and don't use it just for reheating and defrosting. For both fast and low-fat cooking it is invaluable – and cleaning up is a breeze!

- Leftover cooked rice and pasta both freeze well and can be reheated quickly and easily in your microwave oven.

High in fibre, low in fat – microwave popcorn is the ideal snack.

- Microwave popcorn is a low-fat, high-fibre snack. Place 1/4 cup (65g) popping corn in a plain paper or oven bag. Secure bag loosely with kitchen string. Place on microwave turntable and cook on MEDIUM-HIGH (70%) for 5 minutes or until popped. Remove bag from oven with tongs and stand for 2 minutes before opening. Sprinkle with a little salt to serve.

- For tabbouleh in a flash, place 1/2 cup (80g) burghul in a microwave-safe bowl and cover with hot water. Cook, uncovered, on HIGH (100%) for 1 minute. Stand, covered, 1 minute, then drain burghul well on absorbent paper.

- To make cutting and peeling pumpkin easier, place 500g piece of pumpkin on microwave turntable and cook, uncovered, on HIGH (100%) for 2 minutes.

- Corn on the cob tastes freshly picked if you simply place an unhusked cob on the turntable and microwave, uncovered, on HIGH (100%) for about 4 minutes.

- When reheating meals from the fridge, try using a lower heat setting. It may take a little longer, but food will heat up more evenly.

- To cook pappadams without frying, place two at a time on microwave turntable and cook, uncovered, on HIGH (100%) about 30 seconds or until puffed.

Freezer know-how

Many of the recipes in this book are suitable to freeze, or can be made a day ahead, allowing you to prepare ahead for greater time saving.

A baked potato makes a delicious, healthy, light meal.

Precious timesavers

- Use bottled crushed garlic, minced ginger, chopped chilli, and so on, rather than starting afresh each time; or freeze appropriate quantities when you have excess.

- Ask the butcher to trim all visible fat and chop your meat purchases for you.

- For a satisfying, low-fat snack, prick a scrubbed, medium-sized (200g) unpeeled potato several times and cook, uncovered, on HIGH (100%) for 4 to 5 minutes. Top with an accompaniment, such as low-fat cottage cheese and herbs. If you prefer a crisp skin, place microwaved potato in a hot oven for several minutes until crisp.

FROZEN FOOD STORAGE TIMES

meat and poultry	4 to 6 months
minced meat or poultry	2 months
fish: oily	3 months
white	6 months
shellfish	2 months
fruit and vegetables	6 months
cooked pasta or rice	2 months
cream, cheese, milk	2 to 3 months
butter, margarine	6 months
casseroles, soups, pies	3 months
cakes, biscuits, breads	3 to 4 months
eggs (whole, yolks or whites without shell)	6 months

On the table in 30 minutes

You've rushed in late and everyone is *starving*! But you'd still like to serve a healthy, home-cooked meal rather than resorting to takeaway ... again. Help is at hand. All the mouth-watering meals in this chapter can be cooked and served in half an hour or less, and all are also low in fat – proving once and for all that fast food doesn't have to be junk food.

Moroccan beef salad with couscous

1 cup (250ml) vegetable stock
1¹/₂ cups (300g) couscous
500g beef rump steak
¹/₂ cup (75g) dried apricots, sliced
¹/₂ cup (80g) sultanas
1 medium (170g) red onion,
   sliced thinly
¹/₄ cup finely chopped fresh
   mint leaves
2 tablespoons finely chopped fresh dill
1 tablespoon pine nuts
2 teaspoons cumin seeds
³/₄ cup (180ml) oil-free
   French dressing

Bring stock to boil in large pan; remove from heat. Add couscous to pan, cover, stand about 5 minutes or until stock is absorbed.

Meanwhile, cook beef on heated oiled griddle (or grill or barbecue) until browned both sides and cooked as desired; slice beef thinly.

Fluff couscous with fork, add apricots, sultanas, onion and herbs; mix gently.

Place pine nuts and cumin in dry small pan; stir over low heat until seeds are just fragrant and pine nuts are toasted. Combine seeds and nuts with dressing in small bowl; drizzle over beef and couscous.

SERVES 4
Per serve 14.2g fat; 6.3g fibre; 2495kJ.

Spoon from Funkis

Minted lamb and vermicelli soup

100g bean thread vermicelli
1 tablespoon peanut oil
600g lamb fillets, sliced thinly
2 teaspoons bottled chopped chilli
2 tablespoons finely chopped
   fresh lemon grass
2 tablespoons grated fresh ginger
4 cloves garlic, crushed
$1/3$ cup (80ml) fish sauce
1.5 litres (6 cups) chicken stock
1 tablespoon sugar
500g asparagus, trimmed, chopped
$1/4$ cup chopped fresh coriander leaves
$1/3$ cup chopped fresh mint leaves
8 green onions, chopped finely
4 medium (760g) tomatoes,
   seeded, sliced

Plates from Empire Homewares

Chicken, corn and noodle chowder

**1 medium (150g) brown onion,
   chopped coarsely**
2 cloves garlic, crushed
420g can corn kernels, drained
**750g can small potatoes,
   drained, quartered**
1 litre (4 cups) chicken stock
**375g chicken tenderloins,
   chopped coarsely**
150g fresh egg noodles
2 tablespoons low-fat sour cream

Heat oiled large pan; cook onion and garlic, stirring, until onion softens. Add corn, potato and stock, bring to boil; simmer, covered, 10 minutes. Blend or process potato mixture, in batches, until smooth. Return potato mixture to same pan, add chicken and noodles; simmer, uncovered, about 10 minutes or until chicken is tender. Serve with sour cream, topped with finely sliced fresh herbs, if desired.

SERVES 4

Per serve 7.5g fat; 5.9g fibre; 1469kJ.

Place vermicelli in large heatproof bowl, cover with boiling water, stand until just tender; drain.

Meanwhile, heat half of the oil in large pan; cook lamb, in batches, until browned all over. Heat remaining oil in same pan; cook chilli, lemon grass, ginger and garlic, stirring, until fragrant. Add sauce, stock and sugar; cook, stirring, until mixture boils. Add asparagus; simmer, uncovered, until asparagus is just tender. Add herbs, onion, tomato, vermicelli and lamb; stir until soup is hot.

SERVES 6
Per serve 11.7g fat; 6.2g fibre; 1613kJ.

Chicken, corn and noodle chowder *(left)*
Minted lamb and vermicelli soup *(below)*
Tomato and borlotti bean soup *(right)*

White bowls from Accoutrement; green plate from Funkis

Tomato and borlotti bean soup

- **2 medium (300g) brown onions, chopped coarsely**
- **2 cloves garlic, crushed**
- **11 large (1kg) egg tomatoes, chopped coarsely**
- **2 cups (500ml) chicken stock**
- **1 tablespoon Worcestershire sauce**
- **2 tablespoons finely chopped fresh parsley**
- **2 x 400g cans borlotti beans, rinsed, drained**

Heat oiled large pan; cook onion and garlic, stirring, until onion softens. Stir in tomato; cook, stirring, about 3 minutes or until tomato softens. Add stock and sauce, bring to boil; simmer, covered, 15 minutes. Blend or process tomato mixture, in batches, until almost smooth. Return tomato mixture to pan, stir in parsley and beans; simmer, uncovered, about 5 minutes or until hot.

SERVES 4
Per serve 0.8g fat; 11.2g fibre; 417kJ.

Fried rice with prawns

Instead of packaged pre-cooked rice, you may wish to cook-ahead 2¹/₂ cups (500g) long-grain rice for this recipe. Spread cooked rice on tray, cover with absorbent paper; refrigerate overnight.

6 dried shiitake mushrooms
500g medium uncooked prawns
1 tablespoon peanut oil
1 medium (150g) brown onion,
  sliced thinly
1 teaspoon sesame oil
1 clove garlic, crushed
1 tablespoon grated fresh ginger
1 medium (200g) red capsicum,
  chopped coarsely
1 medium (120g) carrot, sliced thinly
2 sticks celery, sliced
100g snow peas
500g packet frozen pre-cooked rice
1 cup (80g) bean sprouts
6 green onions, sliced thinly
¹/₄ cup (60ml) oyster sauce
¹/₄ cup (60ml) hoisin sauce
1 tablespoon fish sauce

Place mushrooms in small heatproof bowl, cover with boiling water, stand 10 minutes; drain. Discard stems; slice caps finely. Shell and devein prawns, leaving tails intact.

Heat half the peanut oil in wok or large pan; stir-fry brown onion until soft. Add sesame oil, garlic, ginger and prawns, stir-fry until prawns just change colour; remove from wok. Heat remaining peanut oil in wok, add capsicum, carrot, celery and peas, stir-fry until vegetables are just tender. Return prawn mixture to wok with mushroom, rice, sprouts, green onion and sauces; cook, stirring, until hot.

SERVES 4
Per serve 8.2g fat; 7.3g fibre; 1537kJ.

Pork, pine nut and cointreau risotto

500g pork fillets
1 tablespoon teriyaki marinade
1 teaspoon finely grated orange rind
3 cloves garlic, crushed
1 large (200g) brown onion,
  chopped finely
2 cups (400g) arborio rice
1.25 litres (5 cups) chicken stock
¹/₂ cup (125ml) dry white wine
2 tablespoons Cointreau
150g baby spinach leaves
2 tablespoons pine nuts, toasted
2 tablespoons coarsely chopped
  fresh lemon thyme

Place pork on rack in baking dish; brush with combined marinade and rind. Bake, uncovered, in hot oven 20 minutes. Cover pork, stand 5 minutes; slice thinly.

Meanwhile, cook garlic and onion in heated, oiled large pan, stirring, until onion softens. Add rice, stock, wine and Cointreau, bring to boil, simmer, covered, 15 minutes, stirring midway through cooking. Remove from heat, stand, covered, 10 minutes. Gently stir in spinach, pine nuts, thyme and pork.

SERVES 4
Per serve 7.6g fat; 4.9g fibre; 2572kJ.

Fried rice with prawns *(left)*
Pork, pine nut and cointreau risotto *(above)*

Mushroom, spinach and lemon risotto

2 medium (300g) brown onions, chopped finely
3 cloves garlic, crushed
1 tablespoon finely grated lemon rind
300g button mushrooms, halved
2 cups (400g) arborio rice
1.5 litres (6 cups) chicken stock
1 cup (250ml) dry white wine
300g baby spinach leaves
2 tablespoons coarsely chopped fresh lemon thyme

Heat oiled large pan; cook onion, garlic, rind and mushrooms, stirring, until mushrooms are browned lightly. Add rice, stock and wine, bring to boil; simmer, covered, 15 minutes, stirring midway through cooking. Remove from heat; stand, covered, 10 minutes. Gently stir in spinach and lemon thyme.

SERVES 4
Per serve 1.6g fat; 7.9g fibre; 1916kJ.

Tandoori lamb naan

250g lamb fillets
1 tablespoon tandoori paste
3/4 cup (180ml) low-fat yogurt
4 naan
2 tablespoons chopped fresh mint leaves
1 tablespoon lime juice
100g curly endive
1 (130g) Lebanese cucumber, seeded, sliced finely

Combine lamb, paste and 1/4 cup (60ml) of the yogurt in medium bowl; cover, refrigerate 10 minutes.
Cook lamb on heated oiled griddle (or grill or barbecue) until browned all over and cooked as desired; slice lamb.
Meanwhile, heat naan according to packet directions.
Blend or process remaining yogurt, mint and juice until smooth.
Place lamb, endive, cucumber and yogurt mixture in centre of naan; roll to enclose filling.

SERVES 4
Per serve 6.7g fat; 2.2g fibre; 1274kJ.

White dishes and tea-towel from Accoutrement; tray from Funkis

White plate from Accoutrement

Spicy chicken fried rice

Instead of packaged pre-cooked rice, you may wish to cook-ahead 2¹/₂ cups (500g) long-grain rice for this recipe. Spread cooked rice on tray, cover with absorbent paper; refrigerate overnight.

2 teaspoons peanut oil
2 eggs, beaten lightly
500g chicken thigh fillets, sliced thinly
2 medium (300g) brown onions, chopped finely
1 tablespoon ground cumin
2 teaspoons ground coriander
¹/₄ teaspoon cardamom seeds
1 teaspoon ground cinnamon
2 bird's eye chillies, seeded, chopped finely
2 cloves garlic, crushed
1 large (350g) red capsicum, sliced thinly
115g fresh baby corn, halved lengthways
500g packet frozen pre-cooked rice
4 green onions, sliced finely
2 tablespoons ketjap manis
2 tablespoons coarsely chopped fresh coriander leaves

Heat ¹/₂ teaspoon of the oil in wok or large pan, add half the egg, swirl so egg forms a thin omelette; cook until set.

Transfer omelette to board, roll, cut into thin strips. Repeat with remaining egg and another ¹/₂ teaspoon oil. Heat remaining oil in wok; stir-fry chicken and brown onion, in batches, until chicken is tender. Stir-fry spices, chillies and garlic in wok until fragrant. Add capsicum and corn; stir-fry until just tender. Return chicken mixture to wok with omelette strips, rice, green onion, ketjap manis and coriander; stir-fry until hot.

SERVES 4
Per serve 11.9g fat; 6.1g fibre; 1887kJ.

Mushroom, spinach and lemon risotto *(above left)*
Tandoori lamb naan *(left)*
Spicy chicken fried rice *(right)*

Easy niçoise-style salad

125g green beans
2 x 425g cans tuna, drained
1 large red oak leaf lettuce
410g can bite-size potatoes,
  drained, quartered
250g cherry tomatoes, halved
1 cup (150g) black olives, seeded
1/2 cup (125ml) low-fat
  French dressing
2 teaspoons seeded mustard
1 clove garlic, crushed
2 teaspoons fresh chervil leaves

Place beans in medium heatproof bowl, pour boiling water over beans, stand 5 minutes; drain. Rinse beans under cold water; drain well. Break tuna into large chunks.

Line large serving bowl with lettuce; top with combined beans, tuna, potato, tomato and olives. Mix dressing with mustard, garlic and chervil in small bowl, pour over salad.

SERVES 6

Per serve 4.2g fat; 3.9g fibre; 846kJ.

Chilli prawn and noodle salad

Red and green Thai chillies may be substituted for the Dutch chillies in this recipe.

250g medium cooked prawns
1/4 cup (60ml) lime juice
2 tablespoons sweet chilli sauce
1 red Dutch chilli, seeded, sliced
1 green Dutch chilli, seeded, sliced
2 teaspoons sugar
200g bean thread noodles
2 tablespoons shredded fresh
  mint leaves

Shell and devein prawns, leaving tails intact. Combine prawns with juice, sauce, chillies and sugar in large bowl.

Place noodles in large heatproof bowl, cover with boiling water, stand until tender; drain.

Combine noodles and mint with prawn mixture.

SERVES 4

Per serve 1.4g fat; 1.2g fibre; 887kJ.

Easy niçoise-style salad *(above)*
Chilli prawn and noodle salad *(right)*

Warm pasta salad with mustard mayonnaise

We used farfalle for this recipe but any short pasta may be used in its place.

**1/2 cup (30g) dehydrated
    sun-dried tomatoes**
250g pasta
2/3 cup (160ml) low-fat mayonnaise
2 tablespoons seeded mustard
1 tablespoon lemon juice
2 cloves garlic, crushed
2 tablespoons hot water
250g sliced leg ham
200g baby rocket leaves
**2 small (200g) red onions,
    sliced finely**
**1/4 cup (40g) black olives, seeded,
    sliced coarsely**

Place tomato in small heatproof bowl, cover with boiling water, stand about 15 minutes or until softened; drain. Slice tomato thinly.

Meanwhile, cook pasta in large pan of boiling water, uncovered, until just tender; drain. Cover to keep warm.

Combine mayonnaise, mustard, juice, garlic and water in small bowl; mix well.

Cut ham thinly, combine with pasta, tomato, mustard mayonnaise, rocket, onion and olives in bowl; mix gently.

SERVES 4
Per serve 12.8g fat; 6.3g fibre; 1824kJ.

Scallop and goat cheese salad

8 slices white bread
12 large (360g) scallops
1 medium cos lettuce
1 small (100g) red onion, sliced finely
150g hard goat cheese, chopped
200g low-fat yogurt
1/4 cup (60ml) lemon juice
1 tablespoon seeded mustard
1 clove garlic, crushed

Discard crusts from bread; cut bread into 2cm squares. Heat oiled large pan; cook bread, stirring, until browned all over. Remove from pan.

Cook scallops in same pan until browned on both sides and cooked as desired.

Combine bread, scallops, lettuce, onion and cheese in large bowl; drizzle with combined yogurt, juice, mustard and garlic.

SERVES 4
Per serve 13.3g fat; 2.9g fibre; 1544kJ.

Warm pasta salad with mustard mayonnaise *(left)*
Scallop and goat cheese salad *(below)*
Sesame chicken noodle salad *(right)*

Sesame chicken noodle salad

680g chicken breast fillets, sliced
1 clove garlic, crushed
2 tablespoons sweet chilli sauce
1/2 teaspoon sesame oil
1/4 cup (60ml) rice vinegar
2 tablespoons soy sauce
1 tablespoon lemon juice
1 green onion, sliced finely
2 teaspoons sugar
600g fresh egg noodles
1 medium (200g) yellow capsicum
1 large (180g) carrot
200g watercress, trimmed
1 tablespoon peanut oil
250g asparagus, trimmed, halved
2 teaspoons white sesame
   seeds, toasted

Combine chicken, garlic and chilli sauce in large bowl.

For dressing, combine sesame oil, vinegar, soy sauce, juice, onion and sugar in jar; shake well.

Cook noodles in large pan of boiling water, uncovered, until just tender; drain.

Discard seeds and membranes from capsicum, cut capsicum and carrot into long thin strips. Combine noodles, capsicum, carrot and watercress in large serving bowl; mix well.

Heat peanut oil in wok or large pan; stir-fry chicken mixture, in batches, until browned and tender. Add asparagus to wok, stir-fry until just tender.

Combine chicken and asparagus with noodle mixture, drizzle with dressing, sprinkle with seeds.

SERVES 6
Per serve 8g fat; 4.1g fibre; 1410kJ.

Grilled asparagus, prosciutto and peach salad

3 large (660g) peaches
6 slices (90g) prosciutto
500g asparagus, trimmed
2 tablespoons lemon juice
2 teaspoons extra virgin olive oil
100g mizuna

Cut peaches in half, remove seed, cut each half in half again. Cut each slice of prosciutto in half. Wrap peach quarters in prosciutto, place on oven tray, bake in hot oven about 10 minutes or until prosciutto is crisp.

Meanwhile, cook asparagus on heated oiled griddle (or grill or barbecue) until browned and just tender; drizzle with combined lemon juice and oil.

Place mizuna on serving plates, top with lemon-coated asparagus and prosciutto-wrapped peaches.

SERVES 4
Per serve 4.4g fat; 3.8g fibre; 480kJ.

Tuna bean salad

100g mesclun
425g can tuna, drained, flaked
400g can butter beans, rinsed, drained
1 small (100g) red onion, sliced finely
250g yellow teardrop tomatoes
1/2 cup (125ml) low-fat
 Italian dressing
2 tablespoons coarsely chopped
 fresh parsley
2 tablespoons coarsely chopped fresh
 basil leaves

Line 4 serving bowls with mesclun. Combine tuna, beans, onion, tomatoes, dressing, parsley and basil in large bowl; divide among serving bowls.

SERVES 4
Per serve 2.5g fat; 4.3g fibre; 609kJ.

Grilled asparagus, prosciutto
and peach salad *(left)*
Tuna bean salad *(right)*

Lamb lavash with crunchy chilli glaze

¹/2 cup (125ml) sweet chilli sauce
3 cloves garlic, crushed
¹/4 cup (60ml) beef stock
¹/4 cup (35g) unsalted roasted
   peanuts, chopped coarsely
300g lamb eye of loin
4 pieces lavash
4 cos lettuce leaves
1 green onion, sliced thinly
1 cup (80g) bean sprouts

Combine sauce, garlic, stock and peanuts in small pan; simmer, uncovered, about 5 minutes or until mixture has thickened to a glaze.

Meanwhile, cook lamb in heated oiled medium pan until browned all over and cooked as desired. Remove lamb from pan, cover, rest 5 minutes; cut into thin slices.

Spread 1 piece lavash with a little chilli glaze, top with lettuce leaf. Sprinkle ¹/4 of the onion and ¹/4 of the sprouts across one short end of lavash, top with ¹/4 of the sliced lamb, roll

lavash to enclose filling; cut in half. Repeat process with remaining ingredients. Serve lavash rolls with remaining chilli glaze.

SERVES 4

Per serve 10.2g fat; 6.1g fibre; 1617kJ.

Lamb lavash with crunchy chilli glaze *(above)*
Moreton bay bug and raspberry
salad *(above right)*
Salmon and dill tortellini salad *(right)*

Moreton bay bug and raspberry salad

Any type of crustacean (for example, prawns, crabs or lobsters) may be used in place of the bugs, if desired.

8 (400g) cooked Moreton Bay bugs
2 teaspoons olive oil
1.5kg watermelon
250g rocket leaves
75g raspberries
1/3 cup (80ml) raspberry vinegar
2 tablespoons chopped fresh
   mint leaves
2 bird's eye chillies, seeded,
   chopped finely

Cut bugs in half lengthways, rinse under cold water; drain.

Heat oil in large pan; cook bugs until heated through and lightly browned.

Using a 2cm melon baller, scoop watermelon into balls.

Combine bugs, watermelon, rocket and raspberries in large bowl.

Mix vinegar with mint and chilli in small jug, pour over salad; toss gently.

SERVES 4

Per serve 3.3g fat; 3.6g fibre; 501kJ.

Salmon and dill tortellini salad

You can use a flavoured tortellini of your choice. Mild flavours such as ham and cheese or cheese and spinach are the most suitable.

375g spinach and ricotta tortellini
1/2 cup (125ml) low-fat yogurt
2 teaspoons seeded mustard
1/4 cup (60ml) oil-free Italian dressing
2 teaspoons finely chopped fresh dill
2 tablespoons water
1 teaspoon sugar
415g can red salmon, drained
1 tablespoon drained capers
2 sticks celery, sliced
1 (130g) Lebanese cucumber,
   sliced thinly

Cook pasta in large pan of boiling water, uncovered, until just tender; drain. Rinse under cold water; cool.

Meanwhile, combine yogurt, mustard, dressing, dill, water and sugar in small bowl; whisk until dressing is smooth.

Combine pasta with flaked salmon, capers, celery and cucumber in large bowl. Just before serving, drizzle with dressing.

SERVES 4

Per serve 10.1g fat; 1.2g fibre; 953kJ.

Bowl from White

Chicken and pickled cucumber pitta

250g chicken breast fillet
1 medium (170g) green cucumber
1 tablespoon cider vinegar
2 teaspoons sugar
1 bird's eye chilli, seeded, chopped finely
1 teaspoon soy sauce
1 small butter lettuce
4 pocket pittas

Cook chicken on heated oiled griddle (or grill or barbecue) until browned both sides and cooked through; cool. Slice chicken thinly.

Meanwhile, slice cucumber into long, thin strips with a vegetable peeler. Combine cucumber, vinegar, sugar, chilli and sauce in medium bowl; stand 10 minutes.

Serve chicken, pickled cucumber and lettuce in pittas.

SERVES 4

Per serve 4.7g fat; 3.4g fibre; 1342kJ.

White dish from Funkis

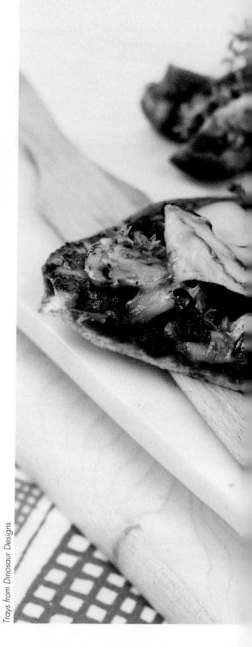

Trays from Dinosaur Designs

Mushroom, eggplant and zucchini pizza

2 medium (240g) zucchini
1 (60g) baby eggplant
200g button mushrooms, sliced thinly
2 large pittas
$^1/_2$ x 140g tub pizza sauce
$^1/_2$ cup (60g) finely grated low-fat cheddar cheese
2 teaspoons finely chopped fresh thyme

Smoked salmon and roasted vegetable lavash

2 large (700g) red capsicums
6 (360g) baby eggplants
4 medium (480g) zucchini
4 lavash
250g rocket leaves
200g sliced smoked salmon
1 teaspoon finely grated lemon rind
2 teaspoons lemon juice

Quarter capsicums, remove and discard seeds and membranes. Roast under grill or in very hot oven, skin-side up, until skin blisters and blackens. Cover capsicum pieces in plastic or paper for 5 minutes, peel away skin; slice capsicum thinly.

Meanwhile, slice eggplants and zucchini lengthways. Place eggplant and zucchini strips, in single layer, on oiled oven trays. Place under hot grill or in hot oven until lightly browned both sides.

Roll each piece of bread into a cone shape; fill with eggplant, rocket, zucchini, capsicum and salmon. Sprinkle with rind; drizzle with juice.

SERVES 4
Per serve 5.1g fat; 9.4g fibre; 1405kJ.

Chicken and pickled cucumber pitta *(far left)*
Mushroom, eggplant and zucchini pizza *(left)*
Smoked salmon and roasted
vegetable lavash *(below)*

Slice zucchini and eggplant lengthways. Cook mushroom, zucchini and eggplant, in batches, on heated oiled griddle (or grill or barbecue) until browned lightly and just tender.

Place pittas on oven trays, spread evenly with pizza sauce. Sprinkle 1/4 of the cheese over each pitta, top with mushroom, zucchini and eggplant; sprinkle with remaining cheese, then thyme. Bake in very hot oven about 10 minutes or until pizzas are browned and crisp.

SERVES 4
Per serve 4.9g fat; 4.4g fibre; 779kJ.

Platters from Bush Wa Zee Ceramics

Chicken and tomato omelette

1/2 cup (125ml) vegetable stock
1/3 cup (20g) dehydrated
** sun-dried tomatoes**
170g chicken breast fillet,
** chopped finely**
1 medium (150g) brown onion,
** chopped finely**
1 clove garlic, crushed
2 eggs, beaten lightly
4 egg whites, beaten lightly
1 tablespoon finely chopped
** fresh chives**

Bring stock to boil in small pan; add tomatoes, simmer, uncovered, about 5 minutes or until tomatoes soften. Drain tomatoes over small heatproof bowl to reserve 1 tablespoon stock; chop tomatoes.

Combine chicken, reserved stock, onion and garlic in oiled 18cm pan; cook, stirring, until chicken is browned. Combine tomato, eggs, egg whites and chives in medium bowl, pour over chicken mixture, cook over low heat about 5 minutes or until egg mixture is almost set, tilting pan occasionally. Place omelette under heated grill for about 3 minutes or until omelette is set and lightly browned on top.

SERVES 2

Per serve 8.2g fat; 1.7g fibre; 978kJ.

Cajun beef roll

500g beef rump steak, sliced thinly
1 medium (150g) brown onion,
** sliced thinly**
1 medium (200g) red capsicum,
** sliced thinly**
2 tablespoons Cajun seasoning
3 medium (570g) tomatoes
1 long French bread stick

Heat oiled large pan; cook beef, in batches, until beef is browned and cooked as desired. Add onion, capsicum and seasoning to same pan; cook, stirring, until onion is browned lightly. Cut each tomato into 8 wedges, add to pan; simmer, uncovered, about 15 minutes or until mixture thickens. Return beef to pan; toss gently to combine with tomato mixture.

Trim ends from bread stick; quarter stick then split pieces almost all the way through. Line bread with lettuce leaves, if desired. Divide beef mixture among bread pieces just before serving.

SERVES 4

Per serve 6.1g fat; 6.8g fibre; 1620kJ (excluding lettuce).

Chicken and tomato omelette *(above left)*
Cajun beef roll *(left)*
Stir-fried mexican beef *(right)*

Platter from Empire Homewares

Stir-fried mexican beef

You can use rib eye (scotch fillet), rump, sirloin or topside in this recipe, if desired.

750g beef eye fillet, sliced thinly
35g packet taco seasoning
1 tablespoon peanut oil
1 large (300g) red onion, sliced thinly
1 medium (200g) red capsicum, sliced thinly
1 medium (200g) yellow capsicum, sliced thinly
4 small (520g) tomatoes, seeded, sliced
2 tablespoons fresh coriander leaves

Combine beef and seasoning in medium bowl. Heat half the oil in wok or large pan; stir-fry beef mixture and onion, in batches, until well browned.

Heat remaining oil in wok, stir-fry capsicums until just tender.

Return beef mixture to wok with tomato and coriander; stir-fry until hot.

SERVES 4

Per serve 13.4g fat; 5.9g fibre; 1449kJ.

Sweet soy chicken and noodles

250g soba
1 tablespoon peanut oil
600g chicken breast fillets, sliced
200g sugar snap peas
2 tablespoons sweet soy sauce
4 green onions, sliced thinly
6 (200g) radishes, sliced thinly
**2 tablespoons finely chopped fresh
    coriander leaves**

Cook noodles in large pan of boiling
water, uncovered, until just tender;
drain. Rinse noodles under hot water;
cover to keep warm.

Meanwhile, heat half the oil in
wok or large pan; stir-fry chicken, in
batches, until tender. Heat remaining
oil in wok, add peas, stir-fry until
just tender. Return chicken to wok
with sauce, onion and radish; cook,
stirring, until hot.

Combine noodles and coriander
in large bowl; serve topped with
chicken mixture.

SERVES 4

Per serve 10.1g fat; 10.1g fibre; 1835kJ.

Stir-fried turkey with lemon and chilli

500g turkey breast fillets, sliced thinly
2 teaspoons finely grated lemon rind
**2 birdseye chillies, seeded,
    chopped finely**
2 teaspoons olive oil
2 cloves garlic, crushed
**1 tablespoon finely chopped fresh
    lemon grass**
**1 large (200g) brown onion,
    sliced thinly**
600g fresh ramen
300g baby bok choy, chopped
2 tablespoons black bean sauce
1/4 cup (60ml) plum sauce
3/4 cup (180ml) chicken stock

Combine turkey, rind and chilli in
medium bowl. Heat 1 teaspoon of
the oil in wok or large pan; stir-fry
turkey mixture, in batches, until
browned and tender.

Heat remaining oil in wok; stir-fry
garlic, lemon grass and onion until
onion is soft. Add noodles and bok
choy; stir-fry until bok choy is just
wilted. Return turkey to wok with
sauces and stock; stir until sauce
boils and thickens slightly.

SERVES 4

Per serve 9.1g fat; 10.1g fibre; 3147kJ.

Sweet soy chicken and noodles *(left)*
Stir-fried turkey with lemon and chilli *(right)*

Bowl and plates from White; spoon from Funkis

Mats from Shack Homewares

Satay pork and noodle stir-fry

500g fresh egg noodles
1 tablespoon vegetable oil
500g pork fillet, sliced thinly
2 cloves garlic, crushed
8 green onions, sliced thinly
3/4 cup (180ml) beef stock
1/3 cup (85g) crunchy peanut butter
1/4 cup (60ml) sweet chilli sauce
2 teaspoons lemon juice
**400g packet fresh Asian-style
    stir-fry vegetables**

Place noodles in large heatproof bowl,
cover with boiling water, stand until
just tender; drain.

Heat half the oil in wok or large pan,
stir-fry pork, in batches, until browned.
Heat remaining oil in wok, add garlic
and onion, stir-fry until soft.

Add stock, peanut butter, sauce and
juice, simmer, uncovered, 1 minute.
Return pork to wok with vegetables and
noodles, cook, stirring, until hot.

SERVES 6

Per serve 12.7g fat; 3.3g fibre; 1368kJ.

Stir-fried prawns and noodles

500g medium uncooked prawns
200g dried rice noodles
1 clove garlic, crushed
2 tablespoons soy sauce
2 tablespoons fish sauce
1 teaspoon sambal oelek
1 cup (80g) bean sprouts
1/4 cup fresh coriander leaves

Shell and devein prawns, leaving
tails intact.

Place noodles in large heatproof
bowl, cover with boiling water, stand
until just tender; drain. Cover to
keep warm.

Heat oiled wok or large pan;
stir-fry prawns and garlic until
prawns are just changed in colour.
Add noodles, sauces and sambal;
gently stir-fry until hot. Stir in
sprouts and leaves.

SERVES 4

Per serve 1g fat; 1.6g fibre; 806kJ.

White platter and chopstick rest from Empire Homewares

Chicken chilli stir-fry

500g chicken breast fillets, sliced
3 birdseye chillies, seeded, sliced
1 clove garlic, crushed
300g snow peas
1 large (350g) red capsicum, sliced
1/4 cup (60ml) oyster sauce
2 tablespoons sliced fresh basil leaves
1 1/2 cups (120g) bean sprouts

Heat oiled wok or large pan; stir-fry
chicken, in batches, until browned
and tender. Stir-fry chilli, garlic,
snow peas and capsicum until
vegetables are tender. Return
chicken to wok with remaining
ingredients; stir-fry until hot.

SERVES 4

Per serve 3.4g fat; 3.7g fibre; 861kJ.

Satay pork and noodle stir-fry *(above left)*
Chicken chilli stir-fry *(below left)*
Stir-fried prawns and noodles *(right)*

Mediterranean-style capsicum rolls

6 medium (1.2kg) yellow capsicums
1 medium (150g) brown onion,
    chopped finely
1 clove garlic, crushed
250g asparagus, trimmed,
    chopped finely
1/3 cup (40g) seeded black olives,
    chopped coarsely
1/4 cup (50g) crumbled low-fat
    fetta cheese
2 tablespoons pepitas, toasted,
    chopped finely
1/2 cup (125ml) oil-free
    French dressing

Halve capsicums, remove and discard seeds and membranes. Roast under grill or in very hot oven, skin-side up, until skin blisters and blackens. Cover capsicum halves in plastic or paper for 5 minutes; peel away skin.

Meanwhile, heat oiled medium pan; cook onion and garlic until onion softens. Add asparagus and olives; cook, stirring, until asparagus is tender. Transfer asparagus mixture to large bowl; stir in cheese and pepitas. Divide asparagus mixture among capsicum halves, roll capsicum around filling; place seam-side down on serving plates; drizzle with dressing. Serve with baby spinach leaves, if desired.

SERVES 4

Per serve 5.9g fat; 4.6g fibre; 584kJ (excluding spinach).

Chickpeas with kumara and tomato

1 tablespoon ghee
2 medium (300g) brown onions,
    chopped finely
2 cloves garlic, crushed
2 teaspoons ground cumin
2 teaspoons ground coriander
1/4 teaspoon cardamom seeds
1 teaspoon chilli powder
1 large (500g) kumara,
    chopped coarsely
2 cups (500ml) vegetable stock
1 tablespoon tomato paste
300g can chickpeas, rinsed, drained

Crisp green vegetables with tempeh

Fresh tofu may be used in place of the tempeh, if desired.

1 tablespoon peanut oil
300g tempeh, chopped finely
500g asparagus, trimmed
1 medium (150g) brown onion, sliced thinly
3 cloves garlic, crushed
200g sugar snap peas
200g baby bok choy, halved
2¹/₂ cups (200g) bean sprouts
¹/₄ cup (60ml) soy sauce
¹/₄ cup (60ml) vegetable stock
¹/₄ cup (60ml) mirin
2 tablespoons rice vinegar

Heat half the oil in wok or large pan, stir-fry tempeh until browned; remove from wok. Halve asparagus lengthways.

Heat remaining oil in wok; stir-fry onion and garlic until onion softens. Add asparagus to wok; stir-fry until tender. Add peas and bok choy; stir-fry until bok choy is just wilted. Add sprouts, sauce, stock, mirin and vinegar; stir until sauce boils. Combine tempeh with vegetable mixture in large bowl.

SERVES 4
Per serve 9.6g fat; 9.3g fibre; 812kJ.

Mediterranean-style capsicum rolls *(far left)*
Chickpeas with kumara and tomato *(left)*
Crisp green vegetables with tempeh *(below)*

4 medium (760g) tomatoes, peeled, seeded, chopped
¹/₃ cup (65g) red lentils, rinsed
2 tablespoons finely chopped fresh coriander leaves

Heat ghee in large pan; cook onion and garlic, stirring, until onion softens. Add spices; stir over heat until fragrant. Add kumara, stock, paste, chickpeas, tomato and lentils; simmer, covered, about 15 minutes or until lentils are soft. Stir in coriander.

Serve with low-fat yogurt, extra coriander and couscous, if desired.

SERVES 4
Per serve 7.3g fat; 11.1g fibre; 1095kJ (excluding serving suggestions).

Thai-style chicken and vegetable curry

2 tablespoons finely chopped fresh
    lemon grass
4 kaffir lime leaves, shredded
1 medium (350g) leek, sliced thickly
2 tablespoons Thai-style green
    curry paste
500g chicken tenderloins, halved
2 x 375ml cans evaporated
    low-fat milk
1 litre (4 cups) vegetable stock
2 tablespoons soy sauce
4 small (360g) zucchini, chopped
300g green beans, halved
1/2 small (200g) Chinese
    cabbage, chopped
350g choy sum, chopped

Spinach and pumpkin curry

1kg pumpkin, peeled
1 tablespoon ghee
2 medium (300g) brown onions,
    sliced thinly
2 cloves garlic, crushed
1 teaspoon grated fresh ginger
2 green birdseye chillies,
    seeded, sliced
1 teaspoon ground coriander
1 teaspoon ground cumin
1 teaspoon black mustard seeds
1/2 teaspoon ground turmeric
1 1/2 cups (375ml) chicken stock
150g spinach, chopped coarsely
1/3 cup loosely packed fresh
    coriander leaves
1 tablespoon flaked almonds, toasted

Cut pumpkin into 3cm pieces. Heat ghee in large pan; cook onion, stirring, until browned. Add garlic, ginger, chilli and spices; stir over heat until fragrant. Add pumpkin and stock; simmer, covered, about 15 minutes or until pumpkin is tender. Add spinach and coriander; stir, tossing, until spinach has just wilted.

Just before serving, sprinkle nuts over curry. Serve with steamed rice, if desired.

SERVES 4

Per serve 7.4g fat; 5.3g fibre; 686kJ (excluding rice).

Spinach and pumpkin curry *(above)*
Thai-style chicken and vegetable curry *(right)*
Prawn curry *(far right)*

200g baby spinach leaves
1¹/₂ teaspoons coconut essence
2 tablespoons lime juice
**¹/₄ cup coarsely chopped fresh
   coriander leaves**

Heat oiled large pan; cook lemon
grass, lime leaves and leek, stirring,
until leek is soft. Add paste; stir until
fragrant. Add chicken; cook until
browned and tender. Stir in milk,
stock and sauce; simmer, uncovered,
about 5 minutes or until thickened
slightly. Add vegetables; simmer,
uncovered, until vegetables are
just tender. Stir in essence, juice
and coriander.

SERVES 6

Per serve 8.3g fat; 6.5g fibre; 1216kJ.

Prawn curry

1kg medium uncooked prawns
2 tablespoons tikka masala
2 tablespoons mango chutney
¹/₃ cup (80ml) vegetable stock
¹/₂ cup (125ml) low-fat yogurt
**¹/₂ cup coarsely chopped fresh
   coriander leaves**
2 teaspoons lime juice

Shell and devein prawns, leaving tails
intact. Heat paste and chutney in large
pan; cook prawns, stirring, until just
changed in colour. Add remaining
ingredients; stir until combined.

   Serve with pappadum strips, rice
noodles and lime wedges, if desired.

SERVES 4

Per serve 6.3g fat; 0.5g fibre; 863kJ
(excluding serving suggestions).

Tuna with char-grilled vegetables

3 medium (600g) potatoes
2 medium (280g) lemons
2 pickled baby dill cucumbers,
sliced thinly
4 small (600g) tuna steaks
2 teaspoons drained green peppercorns
2 teaspoons drained tiny capers

Boil, steam or microwave potatoes until just tender; cut each potato into 4 slices. Cut each lemon into 6 slices. Cook lemon, potato and cucumber, in batches, on heated oiled griddle (or grill or barbecue) until browned and just tender; cover to keep warm.

Cook tuna on same griddle until browned both sides and cooked as desired; cover to keep warm.

Heat peppercorns and capers on same griddle until hot.

Divide potato among plates, then top with tuna, lemon and cucumber. Sprinkle with peppercorns and capers.

SERVES 4

Per serve 4.7g fat; 4.8g fibre; 1212kJ.

Lemony fish fillets with poached leeks

We used barramundi fillets for this recipe.

2 medium (700g) leeks, sliced thickly
3 cups (750ml) chicken stock
3 star anise
1/2 cup finely chopped fresh
lemon grass
2 birdseye chillies, seeded,
chopped finely
3 dried kaffir lime leaves,
chopped finely
4 medium (1.2kg) fish fillets
cooking-oil spray

Combine leek, stock and star anise in medium pan, bring to boil; simmer, uncovered, until leek is just tender. Drain over heatproof medium bowl; reserve stock.

Meanwhile, combine lemon grass, chilli and leaves in small bowl. Place fish on oven tray, press lemon grass mixture on fish; coat with cooking-oil spray. Bake, uncovered, in hot oven about 15 minutes or until fish is cooked as desired.

Serve fish on poached leek; drizzle with a little reheated reserved stock.

SERVES 4

Per serve 9.4g fat; 5.4g fibre; 1593kJ.

Tuna with char-grilled vegetables *(left)*
Lemony fish fillets with poached leeks *(right)*

Mat from Shack Homewares

Grilled fish cutlets with tangy salsa

We used blue eye cutlets for this recipe.

2 (260g) Lebanese cucumbers, seeded, chopped finely
2 radishes, chopped finely
4 medium (300g) egg tomatoes, seeded, chopped finely
1 medium (200g) yellow capsicum, seeded, chopped finely
1/2 teaspoon Tabasco sauce
1 tablespoon sherry vinegar
4 small (700g) fish cutlets, bone removed

Combine cucumber, radish, tomato, capsicum, Tabasco and vinegar in small bowl.

Cook fish on heated oiled griddle (or grill or barbecue) until browned both sides and cooked as desired. Serve fish with salsa.

SERVES 4

Per serve 4.8g fat; 2.4g fibre; 870kJ.

Pan-fried fish with white wine sauce

We used kingfish fillets for this recipe.

1 tablespoon low-fat margarine
1 medium (150g) white onion, chopped finely
1/3 cup (80ml) dry white wine
1/2 cup (125ml) low-fat cream
1 tablespoon coarsely chopped fresh chervil
4 small (800g) fish fillets

Melt margarine in small pan; cook onion, stirring, until soft. Add wine; simmer, uncovered, until wine is almost evaporated. Add cream; simmer, uncovered, until sauce thickens slightly. Stir in chervil just before serving.

Meanwhile, heat oiled large pan; cook fish until browned both sides and cooked as desired. Serve fish and sauce with potato chunks, if desired.

SERVES 4

Per serve 13.8g fat; 0.7g fibre; 1358kJ (excluding potato).

Salmon with dill and caper dressing

2 tablespoons low-fat sour cream
1 tablespoon drained tiny capers
2 teaspoons coarsely chopped fresh dill
2 teaspoons horseradish cream
1 teaspoon lime juice
4 small (600g) salmon fillets

Combine sour cream with capers, dill, horseradish and juice in medium bowl.

Heat oiled large pan; cook salmon until browned both sides and cooked as desired. Serve salmon with dill and caper dressing.

SERVES 4

Per serve 11.6g fat; 0.4g fibre; 871kJ.

Placemats from Acorn Trading

Grilled fish cutlets with tangy salsa *(left)*
Pan-fried fish with white
wine sauce *(above right)*
Salmon with dill and caper dressing *(right)*

Pan-fried turkey with garlic and thyme

750g turkey breast fillets, halved
1 large (200g) brown onion, sliced
4 cloves garlic, crushed
1/4 cup (60ml) lemon juice
1/2 cup (125ml) evaporated
   low-fat milk
1/2 cup (125ml) chicken stock
1 tablespoon finely chopped
   fresh thyme
330g spinach, chopped coarsely
1 teaspoon cornflour
1 teaspoon water

Heat oiled large pan; cook turkey, in batches, until browned all over and tender. Add onion, garlic and juice; cook, stirring, until onion is soft. Add milk, stock, thyme, spinach and blended cornflour and water; cook, stirring, until sauce boils and thickens slightly. Return turkey to pan with any juices; stir until hot.

Serve with mashed potato and steamed vegetables, if desired.

SERVES 6

Per serve 4.7g fat; 2.3g fibre; 778kJ (excluding serving suggestions).

Char-grilled chicken with mango salsa

A 450g can of mango slices may be substituted for the fresh mango in this recipe.

4 single (700g) chicken breast fillets
120g spinach, shredded finely
1 medium (170g) red onion,
   chopped finely
1 medium (430g) mango,
   chopped finely
1 tablespoon coarsely chopped
   fresh mint leaves
1/4 cup (20g) flaked parmesan cheese
1/4 cup (60ml) sweet chilli sauce

Cook chicken on heated oiled griddle (or grill or barbecue) until browned both sides and cooked through.

Meanwhile, combine spinach, onion, mango, mint, cheese and sauce in medium bowl; mix well.

Serve chicken topped with salsa.

SERVES 4

Per serve 6.3g fat; 3.3g fibre; 1222kJ.

Pan-fried turkey with garlic and thyme *(above)*
Char-grilled chicken with mango salsa *(right)*

Poached chicken with tropical salsa

2 cups (500ml) chicken stock
4 single (700g) chicken breast fillets
1/2 small (400g) pawpaw, chopped
1/2 medium (125g) avocado, chopped
1 cup (170g) chopped watermelon
1 tablespoon lime juice
2 teaspoons Angostura
  aromatic bitters
2 teaspoons shredded fresh
  mint leaves

Bring chicken stock to boil in large
pan, add chicken; simmer, uncovered,
about 10 minutes or until tender.
Remove chicken, pat dry with absorbent
paper; cover, refrigerate until cold.
   Slice chicken; top with combined
remaining ingredients.

SERVES 4
Per serve 9.3g fat; 1.9g fibre; 1168kJ.

Poached chicken with tropical salsa *(left)*
Chicken with red pesto pasta *(below)*
Ginger, chicken and lime patties *(right)*

Chicken with red pesto pasta

We used sun-dried capsicum pesto for this recipe, but any bottled "red" pesto, such as tomato, could be used.

4 single (700g) chicken breast fillets
¼ cup (75g) bottled red pesto
375g spaghetti
1 cup (70g) stale breadcrumbs
⅓ cup finely chopped fresh chives
2 teaspoons seeded mustard
½ cup (125ml) chicken stock

Coat chicken with half the pesto. Cook chicken on oiled barbecue plate (or grill or griddle) until browned both sides and cooked through; cover to keep warm.

Meanwhile, cook spaghetti in large pan of boiling water until just tender; drain. Rinse under cold water; drain.

Heat oiled large pan; cook breadcrumbs, stirring, until browned. Stir in spaghetti with remaining pesto, chives, mustard and stock; cook, stirring, until hot.

Serve spaghetti with sliced chicken, and tomato wedges, if desired.

SERVES 4

Per serve 12.3g fat; 5.4g fibre; 2596kJ (excluding tomato wedges).

Ginger, chicken and lime patties

340g chicken breast fillets
1 tablespoon grated lime rind
1 tablespoon grated fresh ginger
2 teaspoons ground cumin
1 egg white
2 green onions, sliced
¼ cup (35g) plain flour

CHILLI SAUCE

2 medium (400g) red capsicums
1 medium (150g) brown onion, chopped finely
4 birdseye chillies, chopped finely
415g can diced tomatoes
1 tablespoon brown sugar

Blend or process chicken until finely chopped. Add rind, ginger, cumin, egg and onion; process until mixture forms a paste. Using hands, shape mixture into 8 patties, coat in flour; shake away excess flour. Heat oiled large pan; cook patties about 2 minutes each side or until browned. Place patties on oven tray, bake, uncovered, in moderate oven about 15 minutes or until cooked through. Serve with Chilli sauce.

Chilli sauce Quarter capsicums, remove and discard seeds and membranes. Roast under grill or in very hot oven, skin-side up, until skin blisters and blackens. Cover capsicum pieces in plastic or paper for 5 minutes, peel away skin, chop pieces finely. Heat oiled small pan; cook onion and chilli, stirring, about 2 minutes or until onion is soft. Stir in tomato and sugar, simmer, uncovered, 5 minutes; stir in capsicum.

SERVES 4

Per serve 4.3g fat; 3.8g fibre; 901kJ.

Lamb and fetta rissoles

400g lamb mince
1 small (80g) brown onion,
 chopped finely
1 clove garlic, crushed
1/3 cup (40g) seeded black
 olives, chopped
60g low-fat fetta cheese, crumbled
1/2 cup (35g) stale breadcrumbs
1 egg white

Combine all ingredients in bowl; mix
well. Shape mixture into 8 rissoles.
 Heat oiled large pan; cook
rissoles until browned both sides
and cooked through.

SERVES 4

Per serve 6.4g fat; 1.1g fibre; 808kJ.

Light 'n' spicy crumbed chicken

12 (900g) chicken tenderloins
1/3 cup (50g) plain flour
2 egg whites, beaten lightly
1/3 cup (35g) packaged breadcrumbs
1/3 cup (35g) corn flake crumbs
2 teaspoons garlic salt
1 teaspoon lemon pepper

Toss chicken in flour; shake away excess
flour. Coat chicken in egg, then in
combined breadcrumbs, salt and pepper.
Cover, refrigerate 15 minutes.
 Place chicken in single layer on oven
tray; bake, uncovered, in hot oven about
15 minutes or until cooked through.

SERVES 4

Per serve 10.5g fat; 2g fibre; 1873kJ.

Black and white sesame crusted lamb

2 cloves garlic, crushed
1 tablespoon lemon juice
1 tablespoon finely chopped
 fresh parsley
2 teaspoons Dijon mustard
500g lamb eye of loin
1 tablespoon white sesame seeds
1 tablespoon black sesame seeds

Combine garlic, juice, parsley and
mustard in small bowl. Place lamb on
wire rack over baking dish; brush garlic
mixture all over lamb, sprinkle with
combined seeds. Bake lamb, uncovered,
in very hot oven about 15 minutes or
until lamb is browned all over and cooked
as desired. Cover lamb, rest 5 minutes;
cut into slices just before serving.

SERVES 4

Per serve 8.3g fat; 1.1g fibre; 813kJ.

Lamb and fetta rissoles *(left)*
Light 'n' spicy crumbed chicken *(above right)*
Black and white sesame crusted lamb *(right)*

Pork with tomato relish

1 medium (150g) brown onion, chopped finely
1 teaspoon ground cardamom
8 medium (600g) egg tomatoes, halved
¼ cup (50g) brown sugar
¼ cup (60ml) balsamic vinegar
¼ cup (60ml) water
4 medium (720g) pork cutlets

Heat oiled large pan; cook onion, stirring, until soft. Add cardamom, tomato and sugar; cook, stirring, until sugar dissolves. Add vinegar and water, bring to boil; simmer, uncovered, about 20 minutes or until mixture thickens.

Meanwhile, cook pork on heated oiled griddle (or grill or barbecue) until browned both sides and cooked as desired.

Serve pork with tomato relish, and pasta, if desired.

SERVES 4

Per serve 13.5g fat; 2.8g fibre; 1235kJ (excluding pasta).

Peanut pork schnitzels

2 tablespoons peanut butter
2 tablespoons low-fat yogurt
2 teaspoons lemon juice
1 clove garlic, crushed
2 teaspoons honey
1 teaspoon ground cumin
6 small (400g) pork leg schnitzels

Combine peanut butter with yogurt, juice, garlic, honey and cumin in small bowl; mix well. Brush pork with peanut butter mixture; cook pork on heated oiled griddle (or grill or barbecue) until browned both sides and just tender.

SERVES 6

Per serve 13.5g fat; 1.5g fibre; 1010kJ.

Pasta with veal and baby beans

250g instant curly lasagne sheets
1 tablespoon olive oil
500g veal leg steaks, sliced thinly
1 medium (170g) red onion,
   sliced thinly
300g button mushrooms, halved
6 slices (90g) prosciutto
250g frozen whole baby beans, thawed
1 tablespoon finely chopped
   fresh sage leaves
1/4 cup (60ml) balsamic vinegar
3/4 cup (180ml) chicken stock

Break pasta into 5cm squares. Cook pasta in large pan of boiling water, uncovered, until just tender; drain. Cover pasta to keep warm.

Meanwhile, heat half the oil in large pan; cook veal and onion, in batches, until browned. Heat remaining oil in pan; cook mushrooms, stirring, until tender. Return veal mixture to pan; add prosciutto, beans, sage, vinegar and stock, stir until hot.

Place pasta in serving bowls, top with veal mixture.

SERVES 4

Per serve 10.1g fat; 7.5g fibre; 1970kJ.

Pork with tomato relish *(above left)*
Pasta with veal and baby beans *(left)*
Peanut pork schnitzels *(right)*

Crusted lamb mini roasts

2 medium (700g) lamb mini roasts
1 tablespoon seeded mustard
2 teaspoons finely chopped
**   fresh rosemary**
2 teaspoons sea salt

Heat oiled large pan; brown lamb all
over. Place lamb on wire rack in baking
dish; brush with mustard, sprinkle
with combined rosemary and salt.
Bake lamb, uncovered, in hot oven
about 20 minutes or until cooked as
desired. Cover lamb, rest 5 minutes;
cut into thick slices just before serving.

SERVES 4

Per serve 6.5g fat; 0.2g fibre; 903kJ.

Steaks with capsicum salsa

1 small (150g) red capsicum,
**   chopped finely**
1 small (150g) green capsicum,
**   chopped finely**
1 medium (170g) red onion,
**   chopped finely**
1 large (250g) tomato, seeded,
**   chopped finely**
1 tablespoon chopped fresh
**   coriander leaves**
1/4 cup (60ml) oil-free French dressing
2 cloves garlic, crushed
1 teaspoon ground cumin
4 small (600g) beef eye fillet steaks

Combine capsicums, onion, tomato,
coriander, dressing, garlic and cumin
in medium bowl; mix well.
    Cook beef on heated oiled griddle
(or grill or barbecue) until browned
both sides and cooked as desired.
Serve beef with capsicum salsa.

SERVES 4

Per serve 10.1g fat; 2.5g fibre; 1091kJ.

Crusted lamb mini roasts *(left)*
Steaks with capsicum salsa *(right)*

Chicken, lentil and spinach pasta

2 teaspoons vegetable oil
**1 small (80g) brown onion,
  chopped finely**
2 cloves garlic, crushed
150g minced chicken
¹/₂ cup (100g) red lentils
2³/₄ cups (680ml) chicken stock
2 tablespoons tomato paste
250g baby spinach leaves
375g shell pasta

Heat oil in medium pan; cook onion and garlic, stirring, until onion softens. Add chicken; cook, stirring, until chicken has changed in colour. Stir in lentils, stock and paste; simmer, uncovered, about 10 minutes or until lentils are tender and sauce thickened. Add spinach; stir until spinach is just wilted.

Meanwhile, cook pasta in large pan of boiling water, uncovered, until just tender; drain.

Combine pasta and chicken sauce in large bowl; to mix, toss well.

SERVES 4

Per serve 6g fat; 10.8g fibre; 1995kJ.

Pasta with tomatoes, artichokes and olives

2 teaspoons olive oil
**1 medium (150g) brown onion,
  chopped finely**
2 cloves garlic, crushed
¹/₄ cup (60ml) dry white wine
2 x 425g cans tomatoes
2 tablespoons tomato paste
¹/₂ teaspoon sugar
¹/₂ cup (80g) seeded black olives
**390g can artichoke hearts,
  drained, quartered**
**2 tablespoons finely sliced
  fresh basil leaves**
375g spiral pasta
¹/₃ cup (25g) flaked parmesan cheese

Heat oil in large pan; cook onion and garlic, stirring, until onion softens. Add wine, undrained crushed tomatoes, paste and sugar; simmer, uncovered, about 15 minutes or until sauce is thickened. Add olives, artichokes and basil; stir until hot.

Meanwhile, cook pasta in large pan of boiling water, uncovered, until just tender; drain.

Combine pasta with half the sauce in large bowl; toss well. Serve pasta topped with remaining sauce and cheese.

SERVES 4

Per serve 7g fat; 11.3g fibre; 1928kJ.

Pasta with roasted mushrooms and tomato

200g field mushrooms
200g button mushrooms
200g Swiss brown mushrooms
250g cherry tomatoes
1/2 cup (125ml) chicken stock
2 teaspoons garlic salt
375g fettuccine
1/4 cup torn fresh basil leaves
1/4 cup (20g) coarsely grated
parmesan cheese

Cut field mushrooms into quarters.
Combine all mushrooms, tomatoes and
stock in baking dish; sprinkle with salt.
Bake, uncovered, in hot oven, about
20 minutes or until mushrooms are
tender and tomatoes softened.

Meanwhile, cook pasta in large
pan of boiling water, uncovered, until
just tender; drain.

Gently toss mushroom mixture
through pasta; sprinkle with basil
and parmesan.

SERVES 4
Per serve 3.7g fat; 7.5g fibre; 1664kJ.

Chicken, lentil and spinach pasta *(far left)*
Pasta with roasted mushrooms and tomato *(left)*
Pasta with tomatoes, artichokes
and olives *(below)*

Bowl from Bush Wa Zee Ceramics

Beef with red wine sauce and polenta

4 small (600g) beef eye fillet steaks
3/4 cup (180ml) dry red wine
1/3 cup (80ml) redcurrant jelly
1 litre (4 cups) chicken stock
1 1/2 cups (250g) polenta
1/2 cup (40g) finely grated parmesan cheese

Heat oiled large pan; cook beef until browned both sides and cooked as desired. Remove beef from pan; cover to keep warm.

Add wine and jelly to same pan; cook, stirring, until sauce thickens slightly. Cover to keep warm.

Meanwhile, bring stock to boil in large pan, add polenta; simmer, stirring, about 5 minutes or until polenta thickens, stir in cheese. Serve beef with red wine sauce and polenta.

SERVES 4

Per serve 14.6g fat; 2.1g fibre; 2360kJ.

Pasta with fetta and red capsicum dressing

We used rigatoni in this recipe, but any short, macaroni-type pasta may be used in its place.

375g pasta
2 medium (380g) tomatoes, seeded, sliced thinly
1 small (100g) red onion, sliced thinly
1/4 cup fresh flat-leaf parsley leaves
90g low-fat fetta cheese

RED CAPSICUM DRESSING

1 small (150g) red capsicum
1 clove garlic, crushed
1 teaspoon coarsely chopped fresh thyme
1 tablespoon red wine vinegar
1 tablespoon lemon juice
1/3 cup (80ml) vegetable stock

Cook pasta in large pan of boiling water, uncovered, until just tender; drain.

Toss hot pasta with tomato, onion, parsley and Red capsicum dressing in large bowl; sprinkle with crumbled cheese.

Red capsicum dressing Quarter capsicum, remove and discard seeds and membranes. Roast under grill or in very hot oven, skin-side up, until skin blisters and blackens. Cover capsicum pieces in plastic or paper for 5 minutes, peel away skin; chop roughly. Blend or process capsicum and remaining ingredients until smooth. Sieve capsicum dressing into small bowl.

SERVES 4

Per serve 4.6g fat; 6.9g fibre; 1688kJ.

Beef with red wine sauce and polenta (left)
Pasta with fetta and red capsicum dressing (below)

Prepare ahead

With a little foresight and advance preparation, you can take the rush out of rush hour. The recipes in this chapter can all be prepared to near-completion a day or two before needed, then refrigerated. When required, simply add the finishing touches and reheat for a healthy home-cooked meal in minutes – perfect for the family and mid-week entertaining, too.

Hoisin pork kebabs with pancakes

Soak bamboo skewers in water for at least 1 hour before using to prevent them scorching.

750g pork fillet, sliced thinly
1/2 cup (125ml) hoisin sauce
2 tablespoons plum sauce
2 cloves garlic, crushed
11/2 cups (225g) plain flour
11/2 teaspoons sugar
3/4 cup (180ml) boiling water
2 green onions
1 small (130g) green cucumber

Combine pork, sauces and garlic in large bowl, cover; refrigerate at least 3 hours or until required.

Combine flour and sugar in large bowl, add water; stir quickly with wooden spoon until ingredients cling together. Knead dough on floured surface about 10 minutes or until smooth. Wrap dough in plastic; stand 30 minutes. Divide dough into 16 pieces; roll each piece into a 16cm round. Heat small frying pan; dry-fry 1 pancake until browned lightly both sides. Repeat with remaining dough.

Keep cooked pancakes covered to prevent drying out. *[Can be made ahead to this stage. Separate pancakes with plastic wrap, seal in plastic bag; refrigerate until required.]*

Thread pork onto 12 skewers. Cook pork kebabs, in batches, on heated oiled griddle (or grill or barbecue) until browned all over and cooked as desired. *[If it's necessary to reheat pancakes, remove plastic wrap, wrap in foil, bake in moderate oven about 10 minutes or until hot.]*

Meanwhile, finely slice onions diagonally. Halve cucumber lengthways; discard seeds, slice cucumber finely lengthways.

Serve kebabs with warm pancakes, onion, cucumber and extra plum sauce, if desired.

SERVES 4

Per serve 5.5g fat; 6.2g fibre; 2067kJ (excluding extra sauce).

Pea and ham soup with sourdough croutons

2 thick slices sourdough bread
cooking-oil spray
800g ham hock
2 cups (400g) green split peas
2 medium (300g) brown onions, chopped finely
2 medium (400g) potatoes, chopped coarsely
2.5 litres (10 cups) cold water
2 cups (250g) frozen peas
1 cup (250ml) water, approximately, extra

Cut bread into large dice. Lightly coat baking dish with cooking-oil spray, place bread in baking dish, lightly coat with cooking-oil spray. Bake, uncovered, in hot oven, turning occasionally, about 10 minutes or until crisp; cool. *[Can be made ahead to this stage. Store cold croutons in an airtight container.]*

Potato lentil patties

1kg Pontiac potatoes
1/2 cup (100g) red lentils
2 teaspoons olive oil
1 small (80g) brown onion, chopped finely
1 clove garlic, crushed
1 egg, beaten lightly
2 tablespoons finely chopped fresh chives
1 tablespoon finely shredded fresh basil leaves
1/3 cup (25g) finely grated parmesan cheese
1/2 cup (125ml) sweet chilli sauce

Boil, steam or microwave potatoes until soft; drain, mash. Meanwhile, place lentils in large pan of boiling water; simmer, uncovered, about 8 minutes or until tender. Drain lentils, rinse under cold water; drain. Heat oil in small pan; cook onion and garlic, stirring, until onion softens. Combine potato, lentils, onion mixture, egg and herbs in large bowl; mix well. Using hands, shape mixture into 12 patties; refrigerate until firm. *[Can be made ahead to this stage. Cover, refrigerate until required.]*

Place patties on baking-paper-lined oven tray; sprinkle with cheese. Bake in moderately hot oven about 30 minutes or until browned. Serve with chilli sauce, and salad, if desired.

SERVES 4

Per serve 7.7g fat; 9.6g fibre; 1435kJ (excluding salad).

Potato lentil patties *(above)*
Pea and ham soup with sourdough croutons *(right)*
Carrot and lentil soup with caraway toast *(far right)*

Remove and discard rind and fat from hock. Rinse split peas under cold water until water runs clear; drain.

Heat oiled large pan; cook onion, stirring, about 2 minutes or until soft. Add hock, split peas and potato; cook, stirring, 2 minutes. Add water, bring to boil; simmer, covered, skimming surface occasionally, 1 1/2 hours. *[Can be made ahead to this stage. Cover, refrigerate until required.]*

Remove hock from soup, shred half the ham. Discard hock; keep remaining ham for another purpose. Stir frozen peas into hot soup, cook, covered, about 5 minutes or until peas have softened. Blend or process soup, in batches, until smooth. Return soup to pan, stir in shredded ham and extra water, bring to boil; simmer, covered, 5 minutes.

Serve soup with sourdough croutons.

SERVES 4

Per serve 3.8g fat; 11.5g fibre; 1304kJ.

White plate from Hale Imports

Carrot and lentil soup with caraway toast

- **1.125 litres (4 1/2 cups) vegetable stock**
- **2 large (400g) brown onions, chopped finely**
- **2 cloves garlic, crushed**
- **1 tablespoon ground cumin**
- **6 large (1kg) carrots, chopped coarsely**
- **2 sticks celery, chopped coarsely**
- **2 cups (500ml) water**
- **1/2 cup (100g) brown lentils**
- **8 slices (200g) ciabatta bread**
- **1/3 cup (25g) finely grated parmesan cheese**
- **2 cloves garlic, crushed, extra**
- **1 teaspoon caraway seeds**
- **2 tablespoons finely chopped fresh parsley**
- **1/2 cup (125ml) buttermilk**

Heat 1/2 cup of the stock in large pan, add onion, garlic and cumin; cook, stirring, until onion softens. Add carrot and celery; cook, stirring, 5 minutes. Add remaining stock and water, bring to boil; simmer, uncovered, about 20 minutes or until carrot softens. Blend or process soup, in batches, until smooth. Return soup to same pan; add lentils, simmer, uncovered, about 20 minutes or until lentils are tender. *[Can be made ahead to this stage. Cover, refrigerate until required.]*

Place ciabatta, in single layer, on oven tray; toast under hot grill until browned. Sprinkle combined cheese, extra garlic, seeds and parsley over untoasted sides of ciabatta; grill until topping is browned lightly and cheese is melted. Cut in half.

Stir buttermilk into hot soup; serve with caraway toast.

SERVES 4

Per serve 4.5g fat; 15.9g fibre; 1433kJ.

Risotto cakes with basil sauce and pancetta

1/2 cup (125ml) dry white wine
1 medium (150g) brown onion, chopped finely
1 clove garlic, crushed
1 cup (200g) arborio rice
3 cups (750ml) chicken stock
2 tablespoons finely chopped fresh parsley
2 tablespoons finely chopped fresh chives
2 tablespoons finely grated parmesan cheese

1 egg white, beaten lightly
4 slices (60g) pancetta
1 teaspoon cornflour
1 teaspoon water
3/4 cup (180ml) low-fat evaporated milk
1 tablespoon finely chopped fresh basil leaves

Heat 2 tablespoons of the wine in large pan, add onion and garlic; cook, stirring, about 2 minutes or until onion softens. Add rice and remaining wine; cook, stirring, about 3 minutes or until wine is reduced by half. Stir in stock, bring to boil; simmer, covered, 15 minutes, stirring midway through cooking. Remove from heat, stir in parsley, chives and cheese; cool. Stir in egg white. Using hands, shape risotto mixture into 4 patties. *[Can be made ahead to this stage. Cover, refrigerate until required.]*

Place pancetta on oven tray, bake, uncovered, in hot oven about 5 minutes or until crisp; drain on absorbent paper. Break pancetta into pieces.

Heat oiled large pan; cook risotto cakes until browned both sides. Place cakes on oven tray, bake, uncovered, in moderate oven about 10 minutes or until hot.

Meanwhile, blend cornflour with water in small pan; add milk, stir over heat until mixture boils and thickens slightly, stir in basil.

Drizzle sauce over risotto cakes; top with pancetta.

SERVES 4

Per serve 3.6g fat; 2g fibre; 1231kJ.

Gingered prawn and palm sugar rolls

1.5kg medium uncooked prawns
1/4 cup (100g) grated fresh ginger
3 cloves garlic, crushed
2 tablespoons finely grated kaffir lime rind
1/4 cup (65g) finely chopped palm sugar
1/3 cup (80ml) sweet chilli sauce
1/3 cup (80ml) chicken stock
12 sheets rice paper
48 baby spinach leaves
1/2 cup (125ml) light soy sauce

Shell and devein prawns; chop roughly. Combine prawns, ginger, garlic, rind and sugar in large bowl, cover; refrigerate at least 3 hours or until required.

Heat oiled large pan; cook prawn mixture, in batches, until prawns have just changed colour. Place chilli sauce and stock in same pan; simmer, stirring, until sauce boils and thickens, pour over prawns.

Place 1 sheet of rice paper in large heatproof bowl of warm water about 1 minute or until softened slightly. Lift paper from water, place on board, pat dry with absorbent paper. Repeat with remaining sheets. Place 4 spinach leaves on centre of each sheet; top with 2 heaped tablespoons prawn mixture. Fold in top and bottom; roll from side to enclose filling. Serve with soy sauce.

SERVES 4

Per serve 1.9g fat; 2g fibre; 1160kJ.

Risotto cakes with basil sauce and pancetta *(left)*
Gingered prawn and palm sugar rolls *(right)*

Polenta with tomato, asparagus and watercress

2 cups (500ml) low-fat milk
1 cup (170g) polenta
1/3 cup (25g) finely grated
   parmesan cheese
1 medium (120g) zucchini,
   sliced finely
2 (120g) baby eggplants, sliced finely
4 medium (760g) tomatoes,
   chopped coarsely
250g asparagus, trimmed,
   halved lengthways
100g watercress

Heat milk in medium pan, without boiling. Stir in polenta; cook, stirring, about 10 minutes or until milk is absorbed and polenta is soft, stir in cheese. Spread polenta into oiled 22cm slab pan, cover; refrigerate until firm. Using 8.5cm round cutter, cut polenta into 4 circles. *[Can be made ahead to this stage. Cover, refrigerate until required.]*

Heat oiled medium pan; cook zucchini and eggplant, stirring, until vegetables are tender. Stir in tomato; simmer, uncovered, about 5 minutes or until tomato softens.

Meanwhile, place asparagus on oiled oven tray; grill until browned lightly and just tender. Place polenta on oiled oven tray; grill until hot and browned lightly.

Serve polenta with tomato mixture, asparagus and watercress.

SERVES 4

Per serve 3.5g fat; 6.3g fibre; 1085kJ.

Tea towel from The Bay Tree Kitchen Shop; underplates from Inne

Gnocchi with caramelised pumpkin and sage sauce

500g pumpkin
1/4 cup (60ml) chicken stock
1 large (500g) leek, sliced thinly
1 tablespoon brown sugar
1 1/2 cups (375ml) water
2 teaspoons finely chopped
   fresh sage leaves
1/2 cup (125ml) low-fat
   evaporated milk
1kg fresh potato gnocchi

Chop pumpkin into 1cm cubes. Place pumpkin in oiled baking dish; bake, uncovered, in hot oven about 30 minutes or until pumpkin is tender.

Bring stock to boil in large pan, add leek; cook, stirring, until leek softens.

Eggplant, tomato and leek lasagne

3 medium (900g) eggplants
coarse cooking salt
1 large (200g) brown onion,
  chopped finely
4 cloves garlic, crushed
3 large (750g) tomatoes,
  chopped coarsely
2 tablespoons tomato paste
1/4 cup shredded fresh basil leaves
1 tablespoon low-fat margarine
2 medium (700g) leeks, chopped finely
2 tablespoons sugar
4 x 16cm x 30cm (200g) fresh
  lasagne sheets
1 cup (125g) grated low-fat
  cheddar cheese

Cut eggplants lengthways into 1cm slices; place slices in colander, sprinkle with salt, stand 30 minutes. Rinse slices under cold water; drain on absorbent paper. Cook eggplant, in batches, in heated oiled large pan until softened and browned both sides.

Cook onion and half the garlic in same pan, stirring, until onion softens. Stir in tomato, paste and basil; simmer, uncovered, about 20 minutes or until thickened slightly. Blend or process tomato mixture until just combined.

Heat margarine in same pan, add leek and remaining garlic; cook, stirring, until leek is soft. Add sugar; cook, stirring, about 5 minutes or until leek is browned lightly. Cut 1 lasagne sheet to cover base of oiled deep 19cm-square (10-cup) ovenproof dish; place in position. Top with 1/4 of the eggplant, 1/4 of the leek mixture, 1/4 of the tomato mixture and 1/4 of the cheese. Repeat layers 3 times, ending with cheese. Bake, uncovered, in moderately hot oven 50 minutes. *[Can be made ahead to this stage. Cover, refrigerate until required. Reheat in moderate oven about 50 minutes.]*

SERVES 6
Per serve 7.4g fat; 8.8g fibre; 911kJ.

Add pumpkin and sugar; cook, stirring, about 10 minutes or until pumpkin caramelises. Stir in water, sage and milk; blend or process pumpkin mixture, in batches, until smooth. *[Can be made ahead to this stage. Cover, refrigerate until required.]* Return pumpkin sauce to same pan; stir over heat until hot.

Meanwhile, cook gnocchi in large pan of boiling water, uncovered, until just tender; drain. Toss hot gnocchi through hot pumpkin sauce.

SERVES 4
Per serve 3.5g fat; 4g fibre; 2184kJ.

Polenta with tomato, asparagus
and watercress *(left)*
Gnocchi with caramelised pumpkin
and sage sauce *(above)*
Eggplant, tomato and leek lasagne *(right)*

Green plates from Funkis

Herbed chicken kebabs with roasted pecans

Soak bamboo skewers in water for at least 1 hour before using to prevent them scorching.

1kg chicken breast fillets, sliced thinly
1/2 cup finely chopped fresh chives
1/3 cup finely chopped fresh oregano
1/4 cup finely chopped fresh marjoram
4 cloves garlic, crushed
1 tablespoon lemon pepper seasoning
2 tablespoons chicken stock
1/4 cup (30g) chopped pecans, roasted

Thread chicken onto 12 skewers. Combine chives, oregano, marjoram, garlic, seasoning and stock in shallow baking dish; add chicken skewers, mix well. Cover; refrigerate at least 3 hours or until required.

Cook kebabs, in batches, on heated oiled griddle (or grill or barbecue) until browned all over and cooked through. Serve with roasted pecans.

SERVES 6

Per serve 7.8g fat; 1.6g fibre; 966kJ.

Citrus chicken with chickpea salad

4 single (680g) chicken breast
fillets, halved
1 tablespoon finely grated lemon rind
1 tablespoon finely grated lime rind
300g can chickpeas, rinsed, drained
1 medium (170g) red onion,
chopped finely
2 medium (380g) tomatoes,
chopped coarsely
1 tablespoon finely chopped fresh
coriander leaves
1 medium (250g) avocado,
chopped coarsely
1 tablespoon lemon juice

Combine chicken, lemon rind and lime rind in medium bowl, cover; refrigerate at least 3 hours or until required.

Combine chickpeas, onion, tomato, coriander, avocado and lemon juice in medium bowl; mix well.

Cook chicken on heated oiled griddle (or grill or barbecue) until chicken is browned both sides and cooked through. Spoon chickpea salad into serving bowls; top with warm chicken.

SERVES 4

Per serve 14.9g fat; 4.8g fibre; 1480kJ.

Tea towel from The Bay Tree Kitchen Shop; fork from Inne

Fork and placemat from Funkis

Chicken and mushroom pastry parcels

510g chicken breast fillets, sliced thinly
100g mushrooms, chopped finely
1 small (200g) leek, sliced thinly
1/2 cup (125ml) low-fat sour cream
1 tablespoon Dijon mustard
1/2 cup (60g) finely grated low-fat cheddar cheese
2 teaspoons finely chopped fresh tarragon leaves
8 sheets fillo pastry
cooking-oil spray

Heat oiled large pan; cook chicken, in batches, until lightly browned and cooked through. Place mushrooms in same pan; cook, stirring, until lightly browned and tender. Add leek; cook, stirring, until leek is softened. Return chicken to pan with sour cream, mustard, cheese and tarragon; cook, stirring, until combined. *[Can be made ahead to this stage. Cover, refrigerate until required.]*

Cut pastry sheets in half crossways; layer 4 halves together, brushing with water between each layer. Repeat with remaining pastry sheets. Place 1/4 of chicken mixture on one short end of pastry; fold in sides, roll to enclose filling. Repeat with remaining chicken mixture and pastry. Place parcels on baking-paper-lined oven tray, spray with cooking-oil spray; bake, uncovered, in moderately hot oven 10 minutes or until pastry is browned lightly and chicken mixture is hot.

SERVES 4
Per serve 13.8g fat; 2.2g fibre; 1578kJ.

Herbed chicken kebabs with roasted pecans *(above left)*
Citrus chicken with chickpea salad *(left)*
Chicken and mushroom pastry parcels *(above)*

Orange pork medallions with roast vegetables

4 (720g) pork loin medallion steaks
1 tablespoon finely grated fresh ginger
1/4 cup (60ml) Grand Marnier
2 medium (360g) oranges
8 (300g) kipfler potatoes
cooking-oil spray
1 medium (400g) kumara
2 medium (700g) leeks

Combine pork, ginger and 1 tablespoon of the liqueur in large bowl, cover; refrigerate at least 3 hours or until required.

Peel oranges; cut each orange into 4 thick slices. Combine orange slices and remaining liqueur in medium bowl, cover; refrigerate at least 3 hours or until required.

Cut potatoes in half lengthways; place in oiled baking dish. Coat with cooking-oil spray; bake, uncovered, in hot oven 10 minutes. Cut kumara in half crossways; cut each half into 8 wedges, coat with cooking-oil spray. Add kumara to baking dish; bake, uncovered, 20 minutes. Cut leeks in half lengthways; cut each half crossways into 4 equal pieces. Add leek to baking dish; bake, uncovered, about 10 minutes or until all vegetables are browned and tender.

Meanwhile, cook pork on heated oiled griddle (or grill or barbecue) about 5 minutes each side or until browned and cooked through; cover to keep warm. Drain orange over medium bowl; reserve liqueur. Cook orange slices, in batches, on same griddle for 2 minutes each side or until tender.

Serve pork with orange slices and roasted vegetables; drizzle reserved liqueur over orange slices.

SERVES 4
Per serve 4.7g fat; 7.5g fibre; 1802kJ.

Pork loin with water chestnut and mushroom filling

1 small (80g) brown onion
1 birdseye chilli, seeded, chopped finely
100g canned water chestnuts, sliced thinly
100g fresh shiitake mushrooms, sliced thinly
1 tablespoon finely chopped fresh lemon thyme
1.3kg boneless pork loin
15 baby spinach leaves

Slice onion into thin rings. Heat oiled large pan; cook onion, chilli, chestnuts, mushrooms and thyme, stirring, until chestnuts are browned lightly and onion is soft. Cool for 10 minutes.

Silver and glass bowl from Inne

Discard rind and fat from pork. Place pork, cut-side up, on board. Make a horizontal cut through the centre of the meaty eye to create a flap; do not cut all the way through. Open out flap, cover pork with spinach, top with water chestnut filling. Roll pork tightly from a long side; tie with kitchen string at 2cm intervals to make an even shape. *[Can be made ahead to this stage. Cover, refrigerate until required.]* Heat oiled large flameproof dish; cook pork, over heat, until pork is browned all over. Transfer dish to hot oven; bake pork, uncovered, about 1 hour or until tender.

SERVES 6

Per serve 3.8g fat; 1.8g fibre; 1110kJ.

Sourdough, ham and potato bake

6 thick slices (240g) sourdough bread
1 cup (250ml) low-fat milk
410g can tiny potatoes
100g shaved leg ham
1/2 cup (125ml) low-fat cream
1/2 cup (125ml) low-fat milk, extra
1 egg, beaten lightly
2 teaspoons finely chopped fresh
    sage leaves
1 clove garlic, crushed
1 tablespoon finely grated
    parmesan cheese

Cut crusts from bread; discard. Cut bread into large dice. Place bread in large bowl, add milk; stand 5 minutes.

Lightly oil 24cm pie dish. Cut potatoes in half. Arrange half the bread over base of prepared dish; top with half the potato and half the ham. Repeat with remaining bread, potato and ham. Pour over combined cream, extra milk, egg, sage and garlic; sprinkle with cheese. Bake, uncovered, in hot oven about 30 minutes or until browned lightly and set. *[Can be made ahead. Cover, refrigerate until required. Reheat in moderate oven about 20 minutes or until hot, covering with foil midway through.]*

SERVES 4

Per serve 9.6g fat; 2.2g fibre; 1143kJ.

Orange pork medallions with roast vegetables *(left)*
Pork loin with water chestnut and mushroom filling *(above right)*
Sourdough, ham and potato bake *(right)*

Teriyaki beef skewers

Soak bamboo skewers in water for at least 1 hour before using to prevent them scorching.

2 large (600g) red onions
500g beef rump steak, sliced thinly
1/4 cup (60ml) teriyaki sauce
1 tablespoon tomato paste
1 clove garlic, crushed
1 teaspoon brown sugar
2 green onions, sliced finely

Cut red onions in half; cut each half into 6 wedges. Thread onion wedges and beef onto 12 skewers. Combine sauce, paste, garlic and sugar in small bowl; brush sauce mixture over skewers. Cover; refrigerate at least 3 hours or until required.

Cook beef skewers on heated oiled griddle (or grill or barbecue) until browned all over and cooked as desired. Serve beef skewers sprinkled with green onion, and steamed rice, if desired.

SERVES 4

Per serve 8.6g fat; 2.7g fibre; 1042kJ (excluding rice).

Char-grilled octopus with tomatoes and chickpeas

2kg baby octopus
2 tablespoons brown sugar
1/4 cup (60ml) tomato sauce
2 tablespoons barbecue sauce
2 tablespoons Worcestershire sauce
2 tablespoons brown malt vinegar
9 medium (675g) egg tomatoes
2 tablespoons balsamic vinegar
2 tablespoons brown sugar, extra
2 tablespoons water
2 tablespoons finely chopped fresh mint leaves
2 x 300g cans chickpeas, rinsed, drained
1/4 cup finely chopped fresh mint leaves, extra
1/4 cup finely chopped fresh coriander leaves

Discard heads and beaks from octopus; cut octopus in half. Combine octopus, sugar, sauces and malt vinegar in large bowl; mix well. Cover; refrigerate at least 3 hours or until required.

Halve tomatoes lengthways. Combine tomato, balsamic vinegar, extra sugar, water and mint in large flameproof baking dish; bake, uncovered, in moderate oven about 45 minutes or until tomato is soft. Remove tomato from dish, cover to keep warm. Add chickpeas to pan juices in same dish; simmer, uncovered, about 3 minutes or until mixture is thickened slightly.

Meanwhile, drain octopus; discard marinade. Cook octopus, in batches, on heated oiled griddle (or grill or barbecue) until just tender; combine with extra mint and coriander. Serve octopus with roasted tomatoes and chickpeas.

SERVES 6

Per serve 2.6g fat; 3.4g fibre; 1096kJ.

Teriyaki beef skewers *(left)*
Char-grilled octopus with tomatoes and chickpeas *(below)*

Kumara and corn frittata

1 medium (400g) kumara
1 (400g) fresh corn cob
1 large (200g) brown onion,
  chopped coarsely
1 tablespoon raw sugar
4 eggs, beaten lightly
3 egg whites, beaten lightly
1/2 cup (125ml) low-fat milk
1/2 cup (60g) grated low-fat
  cheddar cheese

Chop kumara into 2cm pieces. Discard
husk, silk and ends from cob; cut corn
kernels from cob. Combine kumara,
onion and sugar in oiled small baking
dish; shake dish to coat vegetables
with sugar and oil. Bake, uncovered, in
very hot oven 20 minutes; stir in corn,
bake further 20 minutes or until kumara
and onion are tender. *[Can be made
ahead to this stage. Cover, refrigerate
until required.]* Combine kumara mixture
with remaining ingredients in large
bowl; mix well.
    Line deep 19cm-square cake pan with
baking paper. Pour mixture into pan;
bake in moderate oven about 30 minutes
or until frittata is cooked through.

SERVES 4
Per serve 9.9g fat; 5.6g fibre; 1248kJ.

Chilli beans with spicy tortilla crisps

2 medium (300g) brown onions,
  chopped finely
1 clove garlic, crushed
1 medium (200g) red capsicum,
  chopped finely
420g can red kidney beans,
  rinsed, drained
400g can borlotti beans,
  rinsed, drained
2 x 400g cans tomatoes
4 birdseye chillies, seeded,
  chopped finely
1 cup (250ml) vegetable stock
2 tablespoons tomato paste
2 tablespoons finely chopped fresh
  coriander leaves
2 x 18cm flour tortillas
cooking-oil spray
1/2 teaspoon Mexican chilli powder
1/2 medium (125g) avocado, diced

Heat oiled large pan; cook onion and
garlic, stirring, until onion softens.
Add capsicum, beans, undrained
crushed tomatoes, chilli, stock and
paste; simmer, uncovered, about 1 hour
or until thickened. Stir in coriander.
*[Can be made ahead to this stage.
Cover, refrigerate until required.]*

Cut tortillas into wedges; place on oven trays. Spray wedges with cooking-oil spray, sprinkle with chilli powder; bake, uncovered, in very hot oven about 8 minutes or until browned and crisp.

Serve hot chilli beans with tortilla crisps and avocado.

SERVES 4

Per serve 10.7g fat; 15.7g fibre; 1412kJ.

Roasted red capsicum tarts

2 medium (400g) red capsicums
2 large (400g) brown onions,
   sliced thinly
1/4 cup (60ml) balsamic vinegar
1/4 cup (50g) brown sugar
4 sheets fillo pastry
cooking-oil spray
2 tablespoons finely chopped
   fresh basil leaves
1/3 cup (25g) finely grated
   parmesan cheese

Quarter capsicums, remove and discard seeds and membranes. Roast under grill or in very hot oven, skin-side up, until skin blisters and blackens. Cover capsicum pieces in plastic or paper for 5 minutes; peel away skin. Slice each piece of capsicum into thin strips. *[Can be made ahead to this stage. Cover, refrigerate until required.]*

Heat small pan; cook onion and vinegar, stirring, about 3 minutes or until onion softens. Stir in sugar; cook, stirring, about 5 minutes or until sugar dissolves and mixture thickens. *[Can be made ahead to this stage. Cover, refrigerate until required.]*

Oil four 12cm-round loose-base quiche dishes. Cut pastry to give sixteen 14cm-squares. Place 1 pastry square in 1 prepared dish, spray with cooking-oil spray, top with another pastry square, placing corners just to the right of previous square's corners. Repeat layering, using 4 pastry squares in each pie dish. Place dishes on oven tray; bake, uncovered, in hot oven about 5 minutes or until pastry is crisp. Spoon onion mixture into pastry cases, top with capsicum, sprinkle with basil and cheese. Bake, uncovered, in hot oven about 5 minutes or until hot.

SERVES 4

Per serve 2.6g fat; 2.7g fibre; 666kJ.

Kumara and corn frittata *(above left)*
Chilli beans with spicy tortilla crisps *(left)*
Roasted red capsicum tarts *(right)*

Veal cutlets with warm tomato-caper salsa

4 medium (800g) veal cutlets
2 cloves garlic, crushed
1 tablespoon finely grated lemon rind
1 clove garlic, crushed, extra
1 tablespoon finely grated lemon rind, extra
2 medium (240g) zucchini, chopped coarsely
3 large (750g) tomatoes, chopped coarsely
¹/₄ cup (60ml) chicken stock
2 tablespoons tomato paste
2 tablespoons chopped fresh oregano
2 tablespoons drained tiny capers

Combine veal with garlic and rind in large bowl, cover; refrigerate at least 3 hours, or until required.

Heat oiled large pan; cook extra garlic and extra rind, stirring, until fragrant. Add zucchini, tomato, stock and paste; simmer, uncovered, until vegetables are tender and salsa is thickened. *[Can be made ahead to this stage. Cover, refrigerate until required.]*

Cook veal on heated oiled griddle (or grill or barbecue) until browned both sides and cooked as desired.

Meanwhile, stir oregano and capers into salsa until hot. Serve veal with tomato-caper salsa.

SERVES 4

Per serve 4.5g fat; 4.6g fibre; 957kJ.

Thai beef salad

500g beef rump steak
¹/₄ cup (60ml) lime juice
2 tablespoons shredded fresh mint leaves
150g spinach leaves
2 (260g) Lebanese cucumbers, seeded, sliced
1 tablespoon white wine vinegar
2 tablespoons fish sauce
1 tablespoon brown sugar

Combine beef with juice and mint in medium bowl, cover; refrigerate at least 3 hours or until required.

Heat oiled large pan; cook beef until browned both sides and cooked as desired. Cover beef, rest 5 minutes; cut into thin slices. Combine beef with spinach and cucumber in large bowl. Gently toss combined vinegar, sauce and sugar through beef salad.

SERVES 4

Per serve 8.6g fat; 2g fibre; 954kJ.

Veal cutlets with warm tomato-caper salsa *(left)*
Thai beef salad *(right)*

Tofu and spinach stir-fry

350g firm tofu
1/4 cup (60ml) hoisin sauce
1/4 cup (60ml) oyster sauce
1 tablespoon soy sauce
1 teaspoon finely grated fresh ginger
2 cloves garlic, crushed
2 teaspoons peanut oil
1 large (200g) brown onion, sliced
1 medium (200g) red capsicum,
   sliced thinly
200g snow peas
350g spinach, shredded
420g fresh egg noodles

Drain tofu; cut into 2cm cubes. Combine sauces, ginger and garlic in medium bowl with tofu, cover; refrigerate at least 3 hours or until required.

Heat oil in wok or large pan; stir-fry onion and capsicum until soft. Add peas, stir-fry until hot. Add spinach, and tofu mixture; stir-fry until hot.

Meanwhile, place noodles in large heatproof bowl, cover with boiling water, stand until just tender; drain.

Place noodles in bowls, top with tofu and vegetable mixture.

SERVES 4
Per serve 8.9g fat; 8.5g fibre; 1491kJ.

Seasoned beef fillet

1 medium (150g) brown onion,
   chopped finely
2 tablespoons finely chopped walnuts
1/2 cup (35g) stale breadcrumbs
1/2 teaspoon finely grated orange rind
1 tablespoon dry red wine
1/4 cup (60g) seeded mustard
2 tablespoons chopped fresh chives
500g piece beef fillet
1/2 cup (125ml) orange juice

Heat oiled small pan; cook onion, stirring, until soft. Combine onion, nuts, breadcrumbs, rind, wine, 2 tablespoons of the mustard and chives in small bowl. *[Can be made ahead to this stage. Cover, refrigerate until required.]*

Cut deep pocket in side of beef, place seasoning in pocket; secure with kitchen string. Heat oiled flameproof baking dish; brown beef all over. Bake beef, uncovered, in hot oven about 25 minutes or until cooked as desired. Remove beef from dish, cover, rest 5 minutes; slice thickly. Heat same dish, stir in remaining mustard and juice; cook, stirring, until mixture boils. Serve sauce with beef.

SERVES 4
Per serve 11.4g fat; 2g fibre; 1125kJ.

Tofu and spinach stir-fry *(left)*
Seasoned beef fillet *(right)*

Accompaniments

These accompaniments might be side dishes, but they certainly don't play second fiddle. Indeed, the recipes in this chapter are worth a starring role in their own right – as quick, light meals and snacks, or as part of a vegetarian diet. Easy to prepare, high in fibre and very low in fat – can vegies that look and taste this delicious *really* be good for you as well?

Orange hazelnut beans

500g green beans
1/3 cup (80ml) orange juice
**1/4 cup (30g) chopped
   roasted hazelnuts**

Boil, steam or microwave beans until just tender; drain. Place beans in large bowl; stir in juice and nuts.

SERVES 4

Per serve 4.8g fat; 4.2g fibre; 333kJ.

Mixed tomato and pepita salad

4 medium (300g) egg tomatoes
250g cherry tomatoes
250g yellow teardrop tomatoes
1 tablespoon pepitas, toasted
2 tablespoons torn fresh basil leaves
**1/2 cup (125ml) oil-free
   French dressing**

Cut each egg tomato into 6 wedges, combine with cherry tomatoes, teardrop tomatoes and pepitas in large bowl. Combine basil and dressing in small jug, pour over tomatoes and pepitas; toss gently.

SERVES 4

Per serve 1.5g fat; 3.6g fibre; 222kJ.

Orange hazelnut beans *(left)*
Mixed tomato and pepita salad *(right)*

Roasted baby vegetables in maple syrup

1kg baby new potatoes, halved
400g baby carrots, peeled
500g baby turnips, peeled
500g baby beetroot, peeled
1 tablespoon seeded mustard
1/3 cup (80ml) maple syrup
1 teaspoon cracked black pepper
2 cloves garlic, crushed

Boil, steam or microwave potatoes, carrots, turnips and beetroot, separately, until just tender; drain. Place vegetables in baking dish, pour over combined mustard, syrup, pepper and garlic; shake pan to coat vegetables with maple mixture. Bake, uncovered, in very hot oven about 25 minutes or until vegetables are soft and lightly browned, stirring occasionally.

SERVES 4
Per serve 0.7g fat; 15.3g fibre; 1347kJ.

Beans and sugar snap peas with lemon and capers

300g butter beans
200g sugar snap peas
2 tablespoons drained tiny capers
1/4 cup (60ml) lemon juice
2 tablespoons coarsely chopped fresh dill

Boil, steam or microwave beans and peas, separately, until just tender; drain.
   Heat oiled large pan; cook capers, stirring, until lightly browned. Add juice, peas and beans, stir until vegetables are hot. Stir in dill.

SERVES 4
Per serve 0.6g fat; 3.1g fibre; 167kJ.

Roasted baby vegetables
in maple syrup *(left)*
Beans and sugar snap peas
with lemon and capers *(centre)*
Spiced currant couscous *(right)*

Spiced currant couscous

2 teaspoons low-fat margarine
1 medium (150g) brown onion, chopped finely
2 teaspoons ground cumin
2 teaspoons ground turmeric
2 cups (500ml) water
2 cups (400g) couscous
1/2 cup (75g) dried currants
2 teaspoons finely grated lemon rind

Melt margarine in medium pan; add onion, cook, stirring, until onion is soft. Add cumin and turmeric, cook, stirring, until fragrant. Add water, bring to boil; stir in couscous. Remove from heat, stand, covered, about 5 minutes or until all water is absorbed, fluffing with fork occasionally. Gently toss currants and rind through couscous.

SERVES 4
Per serve 2.7g fat; 5.4g fibre; 1669kJ.

Napkins from Shack Homewares

Stir-fried asian greens

500g asparagus, trimmed
1 medium (150g) brown onion
1 clove garlic, crushed
200g baby bok choy, trimmed
200g baby tat soi, trimmed
1 tablespoon sweet soy sauce
2 tablespoons water

Cut asparagus in half. Cut onion into thin wedges. Heat oiled wok or large pan; stir-fry onion and garlic until onion is just soft. Add asparagus; stir-fry until almost tender. Add bok choy and tat soi; stir-fry 2 minutes. Stir in combined sauce and water, stir until tat soi is just wilted.

SERVES 4

Per serve 0.4g fat; 3.6g fibre; 158kJ.

Roasted capsicum and olive salad

2 large (700g) red capsicums
2 large (700g) green capsicums
2 large (700g) yellow capsicums
1/3 cup (50g) black olives, seeded
1 tablespoon balsamic vinegar

Quarter each of the capsicums, remove and discard seeds and membranes. Roast under grill or in very hot oven, skin-side up, until skin blisters and blackens. Cover capsicum pieces in plastic or paper for 5 minutes, peel away skin and discard. Combine capsicum quarters with olives and vinegar in medium bowl.

SERVES 4

Per serve 1.2g fat; 5.5g fibre; 465kJ.

Two-mushroom salad

300g Swiss brown mushrooms
300g button mushrooms
150g mesclun
1/4 cup (60ml) lemon juice
1 tablespoon seeded mustard
1 tablespoon chopped fresh thyme

Cook Swiss brown and button mushrooms, in batches, on heated oiled griddle (or grill or barbecue) until browned and just tender. Combine mesclun and mushrooms in large bowl, pour over combined juice, mustard and thyme; toss gently.

SERVES 4
Per serve 0.7g fat; 4.7g fibre; 190kJ.

Garlic kipfler potatoes

1kg kipfler potatoes
8 cloves garlic
1 teaspoon salt

Boil, steam or microwave potatoes until just tender; drain. Cut potatoes in half lengthways, place in oiled baking dish with garlic; sprinkle with salt. Bake, uncovered, in hot oven about 45 minutes or until potato is brown and crisp. Squeeze 2 of the garlic cloves over potato; shake gently to combine.

SERVES 4
Per serve 0.4g fat; 5g fibre; 706kJ.

Stir-fried asian greens *(far left)*
Roasted capsicum and olive salad *(back)*
Two-mushroom salad *(far right)*
Garlic kipfler potatoes *(front)*

Eggplant, spinach and butter lettuce salad

1 small (230g) eggplant, sliced thinly
150g baby spinach leaves
1 small butter lettuce
2 (260g) Lebanese cucumbers, seeded, sliced finely
2 green onions, sliced finely
1/2 cup (125ml) oil-free Italian dressing

Place eggplant, in single layer, on oven tray; grill until lightly browned on both sides. Combine eggplant with spinach, torn lettuce leaves, cucumber, onion and dressing in large bowl.

SERVES 4

Per serve 0.5g fat; 4.4g fibre; 175kJ.

Red lentil salad

Lentils can be used warm, or leave to cool before assembling salad.

1¹/2 cups (300g) red lentils
2 teaspoons cumin seeds
2 teaspoons ground coriander
4 green onions, sliced finely
1 clove garlic, crushed
1/4 cup (60ml) lime juice
1/4 cup (60ml) seasoned rice vinegar
1/4 cup finely chopped fresh coriander leaves

Cover lentils with water in medium pan, bring to boil, then simmer, covered, about 10 minutes or until lentils are just tender; drain.
   Heat small pan, cook seeds and ground coriander, stirring, until fragrant.
   Combine lentils with onion, garlic, spices, lime juice, vinegar and fresh coriander in large bowl; mix well.

SERVES 4

Per serve 1.9g fat; 11.5g fibre; 890kJ.

Brandied carrots and leek

1 large (500g) leek
3 large (540g) carrots
1/4 cup (60ml) water
1/4 cup (60ml) brandy
2 tablespoons honey

Cut leek and carrots into 10cm lengths. Heat the water in large pan; cook carrot, covered, about 5 minutes or until carrot is just tender, stirring occasionally. Add leek, cook, stirring, until leek is tender. Add brandy and honey, stir over heat until sauce is syrupy.

SERVES 4

Per serve 0.4g fat; 6.7g fibre; 502kJ.

Eggplant, spinach and butter lettuce salad *(left)*
Red lentil salad *(above right)*
Brandied carrots and leek *(right)*

Napkin from Shack Homewares

Bowl and placemat from Shack Homewares

Low-fat caesar-style salad

1 ciabatta loaf
150g sliced leg ham, chopped finely
1/2 cup (125ml) buttermilk
1 tablespoon lemon juice
1 tablespoon Dijon mustard
1 clove garlic, crushed
1 medium cos lettuce
2 medium (150g) egg
   tomatoes, quartered
1 (130g) Lebanese cucumber,
   sliced thinly

Remove and discard crust from bread,
slice bread into 2cm-thick slices; cut
slices into 3cm squares. Place squares,
in single layer, on oven tray. Bake in
very hot oven about 10 minutes or
until croutons are lightly browned,
turning occasionally; cool.

Heat large pan; cook ham, stirring,
until lightly browned.

Combine buttermilk, juice, mustard
and garlic in small jug.

Combine torn lettuce leaves with
croutons, tomato, cucumber and ham
in large bowl, pour over buttermilk
dressing; mix gently.

SERVES 4

Per serve 4.1g fat; 7.5g fibre; 1215kJ.

Smoky potato salad

1kg tiny new potatoes, halved
200g sliced leg ham
2 cloves garlic, crushed
2 tablespoons cider vinegar
1 tablespoon seeded mustard
2 teaspoons olive oil
1 tablespoon finely chopped
   fresh chives
2 green onions, chopped finely

Boil, steam or microwave potato
until just tender; drain. Cook potato,
in batches, on heated oiled griddle
(or grill or barbecue) until browned all
over. Cook ham, in batches, on heated
oiled griddle until browned both sides;
chop coarsely. Combine garlic, vinegar,
mustard, oil and chives in jar; shake
well. Combine potato and ham
in large bowl; pour over dressing,
sprinkle with onions.

SERVES 4

Per serve 6.4g fat; 4.9g fibre; 1050kJ.

Green pea puree

1/2 cup (125ml) dry white wine
1 medium (150g) brown onion,
   chopped finely
1/2 cup (125ml) chicken stock
500g frozen peas
1 tablespoon finely chopped fresh
   mint leaves

Heat wine in medium pan, add onion,
cook, stirring, about 5 minutes or
until onion is soft and wine reduced
by half. Stir in chicken stock and peas,
bring to boil, then simmer, uncovered,
about 10 minutes or until peas are soft.
Stir in mint. Blend or process pea
mixture, in batches, until smooth.

SERVES 4

Per serve 0.6g fat; 7.9g fibre; 394kJ.

Low-fat caesar-style salad *(left)*
Smoky potato salad *(centre)*
Green pea puree *(right)*

Zucchini, squash and broad bean medley

1 tablespoon low-fat
   margarine, melted
1 teaspoon finely grated
   lemon rind
1 tablespoon lemon juice
2 tablespoons seeded mustard
2 tablespoons finely chopped
   fresh parsley
2 large (300g) zucchini
400g yellow squash, quartered
500g frozen broad beans

For dressing, combine margarine,
rind, juice, mustard and parsley
in small bowl.
   Cut zucchini into 1cm-wide
slices. Boil, steam or microwave
squash, zucchini and beans,
separately, until tender; drain.
Combine hot vegetables with half
the dressing in large bowl; drizzle
with remaining dressing.

SERVES 4

Per serve 3g fat; 11.2g fibre; 466kJ.

Coleslaw with fat-free dressing

We used crinkly savoy cabbage for this recipe.

1/2 small (600g) cabbage, sliced finely
1 large (180g) carrot, grated coarsely
4 green onions, sliced thinly
2 sticks (300g) celery, sliced thinly
1/4 cup (60ml) white wine vinegar
2 tablespoons seeded mustard

Combine cabbage, carrot, onion and celery in large bowl. Combine vinegar and mustard in small bowl, pour over vegetables; toss well.

SERVES 4

Per serve 0.6g fat; 7.9g fibre; 225kJ.

Snake bean and asparagus salad with citrus dressing

500g asparagus, trimmed
200g snake beans, trimmed
2 small (260g) tomatoes, chopped finely
1 small (100g) red onion, chopped finely
2 cloves garlic, crushed
1 tablespoon lemon juice
2 tablespoons orange juice
1 tablespoon cider vinegar

Slice asparagus and beans into 6cm-lengths. Place asparagus in large pan of boiling water; drain immediately. Place beans in large pan of boiling water; drain immediately. Combine asparagus, beans, tomato and onion in large bowl. Combine garlic, juices and vinegar in small jug; pour over salad just before serving.

SERVES 4

Per serve 0.4g fat; 4.1g fibre; 196kJ.

Zucchini, squash and broad bean medley *(left)*
Coleslaw with fat-free dressing *(centre)*
Snake bean and asparagus salad with citrus dressing *(right)*

Pink-eye potato crisps

4 medium (425g) pink-eye potatoes
cooking oil spray

Slice unpeeled potato thinly, rinse
well, pat dry with absorbent paper.
Line oven trays with baking paper,
place slices, in single layer, on trays;
spray with oil. Bake in hot oven about
20 minutes or until crisps are browned
and crunchy.

SERVES 4

Per serve 0.1g fat; 1.7g fibre; 290kJ.

Pink-eye potato crisps *(left)*
Crunchy baked rosti *(centre left)*
Kipfler potato cakes *(centre right)*
Mixed vegetables with honey glaze *(right)*

Kipfler potato cakes

1kg kipfler potatoes, peeled
1 clove garlic, crushed
1 teaspoon lemon pepper seasoning
$1/2$ cup (60g) finely grated low-fat
    cheddar cheese
2 tablespoons low-fat sour cream

Boil, steam or microwave potato
until just tender; drain. Mash potato;
combine with remaining ingredients
in large bowl, cool. Using hands,
shape 1/3 cup of mixture into a patty;
repeat with remaining mixture. Cook
patties, in batches, in heated oiled
large pan until lightly browned both
sides and heated through.

SERVES 4

Per serve 5.9g fat; 4.3g fibre; 986kJ.

Square plate from The Bay Tree Kitchen Shop

Mixed vegetables with honey glaze

400g baby carrots
200g sugar snap peas
120g corn spears, halved
1 tablespoon low-fat margarine
1/4 cup (60ml) orange juice
2 tablespoons honey

Boil, steam or microwave carrot, peas and corn, separately, until just tender; drain. Melt margarine in large pan; add carrot, peas, corn, juice and honey, stir until vegetables are hot and glaze is syrupy.

SERVES 4
Per serve 2.5g fat; 5.4g fibre; 557kJ.

Crunchy baked rosti

2 medium (400g) potatoes, peeled
1 teaspoon low-fat margarine
1 medium (350g) leek, sliced thinly
2 cloves garlic, crushed
1/2 teaspoon sweet paprika
1/4 cup (20g) finely grated
   parmesan cheese

Boil, steam or microwave potato until just tender; drain, cool. Coarsely grate potato. Melt margarine in large pan; cook leek, garlic and paprika, stirring, until leek is lightly browned. Combine leek mixture, potato and cheese in

medium bowl. Place 7.5cm egg ring on baking-paper-covered oven tray, press 1/4 cup of potato mixture into ring; gently remove ring. Repeat with remaining potato mixture. Bake in very hot oven about 20 minutes or until browned.

SERVES 4
Per serve 2.5g fat; 3.5g fibre; 449kJ.

Bowls from Hale Imports

Fetta, olive and rocket salad with roasted tomatoes

6 medium (450g) egg tomatoes
2 tablespoons brown sugar
2 tablespoons balsamic vinegar
2 teaspoons Dijon mustard
1 tablespoon brown sugar, extra
250g baby rocket
1 large (300g) red onion, chopped finely
1/3 cup (50g) black olives, seeded, sliced finely
60g low-fat fetta cheese, crumbled

Cut tomatoes in half lengthways. Place tomatoes, cut-side up, on oven tray, sprinkle with sugar. Bake, uncovered, in hot oven about 10 minutes or until just tender.

For dressing, combine vinegar, mustard and extra sugar in small jug.

Just before serving, combine rocket, onion, olives and tomato in large bowl, drizzle dressing over salad, scatter with cheese.

SERVES 4

Per serve 2.9g fat; 4.3g fibre; 566kJ.

White beans in rich tomato sauce

1 medium (150g) brown onion, chopped finely
2 cloves garlic, crushed
415g can tomato puree
2 x 400g cans cannellini beans, rinsed, drained
1 tablespoon finely sliced fresh flat-leaf parsley

Heat oiled medium pan, add onion and garlic, cook, stirring, until onion is soft. Stir in tomato puree and beans, simmer, uncovered, until thickened slightly. Stir in parsley.

SERVES 4

Per serve 1g fat; 11g fibre; 556kJ.

Pumpkin and parsnip bake

750g pumpkin
2 large (360g) parsnips
1 clove garlic, crushed
cooking oil spray
1 tablespoon low-fat margarine, melted
1 cup stale breadcrumbs

Peel pumpkin, discard seeds, cut pumpkin into large dice. Peel parsnips; cut parsnips into large dice. Combine pumpkin, parsnip and garlic in large baking dish, lightly coat vegetables with cooking-oil spray. Bake, uncovered, in hot oven about 30 minutes or until vegetables are lightly browned and tender. Sprinkle with combined margarine and breadcrumbs; toss through gently. Bake about 10 minutes or until breadcrumbs are golden brown.

SERVES 4

Per serve 3.3g fat; 4.7g fibre; 702kJ.

White plates and dishes from Hale Imports

Fetta, olive and rocket salad with roasted tomatoes *(above left)*
White beans in rich tomato sauce *(left)*
Pumpkin and parsnip bake *(right)*

Bacon, buttermilk and chive mash

2 bacon rashers
4 large (1.2kg) potatoes, halved
1/2 cup (125ml) buttermilk
2 tablespoons finely chopped fresh chives

Discard fat from bacon, chop bacon finely. Heat small pan, cook bacon, stirring, until crisp; drain on absorbent paper.

Meanwhile, boil, steam or microwave potato until just tender; drain. Push potato through sieve into large bowl; stir in bacon, buttermilk and chives.

SERVES 4

Per serve 3.4g fat; 5.8g fibre; 1165kJ.

Tomato and basil potatoes

1kg tiny new potatoes, halved
cooking oil spray
1 medium (150g) brown onion, sliced thinly
2 cloves garlic, crushed
2 medium (380g) tomatoes, seeded, sliced thinly
1 tablespoon white wine vinegar
3/4 cup (180ml) tomato juice
1/2 teaspoon sugar
2 tablespoons small fresh basil leaves

Boil, steam or microwave potato until just tender; drain. Place potato in baking dish, spray with cooking oil, bake, uncovered, in very hot oven about 30 minutes or until lightly browned.

Just before serving, cook onion in large pan, stirring, until soft. Add garlic, tomato, vinegar, juice and sugar, bring to boil, then simmer, uncovered, about 5 minutes or until sauce thickens. Combine potato with tomato mixture in large bowl; mix in basil leaves.

SERVES 4

Per serve 0.4g fat; 6.4g fibre; 806kJ.

Wild rice salad

1 cup (180g) wild rice
2 cups (400g) brown rice
2 sticks celery, sliced finely
310g can corn kernels, drained
4 medium (760g) tomatoes, seeded, sliced thinly
2/3 cup (160ml) oil-free French dressing
2 cloves garlic, crushed
1/3 cup finely chopped fresh flat-leaf parsley

Cook wild rice in large pan of boiling water, uncovered, until just tender; drain. Rinse under cold water; drain.

Meanwhile, cook brown rice in another large pan of boiling water, uncovered, until just tender; drain. Rinse under cold water; drain.

Combine wild rice and brown rice in large bowl with celery, corn and tomato. Add combined dressing, garlic and parsley; mix well.

SERVES 6

Per serve 2.9g fat; 2.1g fibre; 1700kJ.

Bacon, buttermilk and chive mash *(below left)*
Tomato and basil potatoes *(below right)*
Wild rice salad *(right)*

Desserts

Go on, indulge yourself a little. These dazzling desserts – some ready in minutes, others suitable to prepare ahead – will satisfy the sweetest tooth without adding to your waistline. Fruit features, of course, but there are also creamy mousses and custard, melt-in-the-mouth meringues, delectable pastries and even – bliss! – a touch of chocolate.

Vanilla ricotta mousse

Can be partially prepared ahead.

100g low-fat ricotta cheese
**2 x 125g tubs light French
    vanilla Fruche**
1/2 cup (110g) caster sugar
1 teaspoon vanilla essence
1 teaspoon gelatine
1/2 cup (125ml) water
1 cup (250ml) sweet dessert wine
1 vanilla bean, split

Lightly grease four 1/2-cup (125ml) shallow dishes. Blend or process ricotta, Fruche, 1 tablespoon of the sugar and essence until smooth. Sprinkle gelatine over 1 tablespoon of the water in cup, stand cup in pan of simmering water, stir until gelatine is dissolved. Stir gelatine through ricotta mixture, pour evenly into prepared dishes, cover; refrigerate about 30 minutes or until set. *[Can be kept in refrigerator up to 2 days.]*

Combine remaining sugar, remaining water, wine and vanilla bean in small pan; stir over heat, without boiling, until sugar dissolves. Bring to boil; simmer about 5 minutes or until syrup thickens. Remove and discard bean; let syrup cool.

Just before serving, turn mousse onto plates; serve with wine syrup.

SERVES 4

Per serve 2.2g fat; 0.02g fibre; 982kJ.

French meringues with berries

Can be partially prepared ahead.

2 egg whites
1 teaspoon lemon juice
1/2 cup (110g) caster sugar
**1/3 cup (50g) shelled pistachios,
    chopped finely**
200g tub low-fat strawberry Fruche
75g fresh raspberries
75g fresh blueberries

Beat egg whites and juice in small bowl with electric mixer until soft peaks form. Add sugar, in batches, beating until dissolved between additions.

Line 3 oven trays with baking paper, trace twelve 5.5cm circles onto each sheet of baking paper. Spread meringue thinly over circles on paper, sprinkle with nuts; bake in very slow oven about 30 minutes or until crisp. Cool in oven with door ajar. *[Can be made ahead to this stage. Store in airtight container up to 3 days.]*

Divide Fruche among 18 of the meringues, decorate with raspberries and blueberries; top with remaining meringues. Decorate with extra berries, if desired.

MAKES 18

Per meringue 0.7g fat; 0.3g fibre; 112kJ (excluding extra berries).

Vanilla ricotta mousse *(left)*
French meringues with berries *(right)*

Lime and lemon grass mangoes

2 cups (440g) sugar
2 cups (500ml) water
1 tablespoon finely grated lime rind
1/4 cup (60ml) lime juice
10cm piece fresh lemon grass,
    sliced finely
2 kaffir lime leaves, sliced finely
4 large (2.4kg) mangoes

Combine sugar, water, rind, juice, lemon grass and lime leaves in medium pan; stir, over low heat, until sugar dissolves. Bring to boil; simmer, uncovered, about 15 minutes or until syrup has thickened slightly.

Meanwhile, cut through mango lengthways, on each side of seed, to give 2 cheeks; peel away skin. Place mango cheeks in large heatproof bowl; pour syrup over mango, serve warm or cold.

SERVES 4

Per serve 0.9g fat; 6.5g fibre; 2788kJ.

Grilled nashi with rosewater syrup

2 cups (500ml) water
3/4 cup (165g) caster sugar
2 1/2 teaspoons rosewater
4 medium (1kg) nashi, halved
1 tablespoon honey
1 tablespoon brown sugar

Combine water, caster sugar and rosewater in medium pan; stir over heat, without boiling, until sugar dissolves. Add nashi; simmer, uncovered, about 10 minutes or until nashi are tender.

Drain nashi over large heatproof bowl; reserve syrup, cover to keep warm. Place nashi on oven tray, drizzle with honey, sprinkle with brown sugar. Grill nashi until sugar dissolves. Serve nashi warm or cold with warm rosewater syrup.

SERVES 4

Per serve 0.3g fat; 5.8g fibre; 1339kJ.

Fresh fruit with passionfruit yogurt

You will need about 2 passionfruit for this recipe.

1/4 medium (600g) rockmelon
1/2 medium (600g) pineapple
4 medium (450g) plums
4 medium (240g) fresh figs, sliced
200ml low-fat yogurt
2 tablespoons passionfruit pulp
1/4 cup (60ml) honey

Chop rockmelon, pineapple and plums into bite-size pieces; place in serving bowls. Add fig, top with yogurt; drizzle with passionfruit and honey.

SERVES 4
Per serve 1.3g fat; 7.3g fibre; 843kJ.

Raspberries and watermelon with hazelnut syrup

Use fresh or frozen raspberries in this recipe.

1.5kg watermelon
150g raspberries
1/4 cup shredded fresh mint leaves
1/2 cup (125ml) lemon juice
2 tablespoons raw sugar
**1/3 cup (40g) coarsely chopped
    roasted hazelnuts**

Discard watermelon rind; chop watermelon into large pieces. Combine watermelon, raspberries and mint in large heatproof bowl.
    Combine juice, sugar and nuts in small pan; stir, over low heat, until sugar is dissolved. Bring to boil. Pour hot syrup over watermelon mixture.

SERVES 4
Per serve 6.8g fat; 4.7g fibre; 713kJ.

Lime and lemon grass mangoes *(above left)*
Grilled nashi with rosewater syrup *(left)*
Fresh fruit with passionfruit yogurt *(above right)*
Raspberries and watermelon
with hazelnut syrup *(right)*

Glass bowl and spoon from Wednesdays Homewares; glass plate from Accoutrement

Fruit with creamy chocolate dip

Tia Maria is a coffee-flavoured liqueur; you can use Kahlua as a substitute.

250g cottage cheese
200ml low-fat vanilla yogurt
2 teaspoons cocoa powder
$1/2$ cup (100g) firmly packed brown sugar
2 tablespoons Tia Maria
250g strawberries
2 large (460g) bananas
2 large (400g) red apples

Blend or process cheese, yogurt, cocoa, sugar and liqueur until smooth. Spoon into serving bowl, cover; refrigerate 30 minutes.

Just before serving, cut strawberries in half; slice bananas and apples into bite-size pieces. Serve fruit with dip.

SERVES 4

Per serve 6.5g fat; 5.2g fibre; 1584kJ.

Chocolate and ice-cream fillo sandwiches

4 sheets fillo pastry
cooking-oil spray
1 egg white, beaten lightly
1 tablespoon shelled pistachios, chopped finely
2 teaspoons caster sugar
$1/4$ teaspoon ground cinnamon
400g low-fat vanilla ice-cream
$1/2$ cup (125ml) diet chocolate topping

Stack fillo sheets together, spraying between each layer with cooking-oil spray. Cut fillo stack in half lengthways, then cut each half into quarters crossways; you will have 8 rectangular fillo stacks in all. Place stacks on greased oven trays. Brush 4 stacks with egg white, sprinkle with nuts, then combined sugar and cinnamon. Bake all stacks in hot oven about 5 minutes or until golden brown and crisp.

Just before serving, place 1 of the plain stacks on each plate, top with scoops of ice-cream, drizzle with topping; sandwich with remaining stacks.

SERVES 4

Per serve 5.1g fat; 0.6g fibre; 369kJ.

Fruit with creamy chocolate dip *(above left)*
Chocolate and ice-cream fillo sandwiches *(left)*
Watermelon mint ice *(above right)*
Sparkling lime granita *(below right)*

Placemats from Accoutrement

Sparkling lime granita

Can be partially prepared ahead. You will need about 6 large limes for this recipe; grate rind before squeezing juice. We used a sparkling pinot noir chardonnay for this recipe, but any sparkling white wine may be used.

1/2 cup (110g) caster sugar
1/4 cup (60ml) water
1/2 cup (125ml) fresh lime juice
2 cups (500ml) sparkling white wine
2 tablespoons finely grated lime rind
1 egg white, beaten lightly

Combine sugar, water and juice in small pan; cook, stirring, over low heat until sugar dissolves. Bring to boil; simmer, uncovered, 5 minutes. Stir in wine and rind. Pour mixture into loaf pan, cover with foil; freeze until just firm. *[Can be frozen up to 2 days.]*

Chop mixture, place in large bowl of electric mixer; beat in egg white until combined. Return to pan, cover; freeze until firm.

SERVES 4
Per serve 0.07g fat; 0.2g fibre; 846kJ.

Watermelon mint ice

Can be prepared ahead.

1.5kg watermelon
1/2 cup (110g) caster sugar
1 cup (250ml) water
1/4 cup coarsely chopped fresh mint leaves
2 egg whites, beaten lightly
1 teaspoon finely chopped fresh mint leaves, extra

Discard watermelon rind; blend or process watermelon until smooth. Push watermelon through sieve into large bowl; discard pulp. You need 2 1/2 cups (625ml) watermelon juice for this recipe.

Combine sugar, the water and mint in medium pan; stir over heat, without boiling, until sugar dissolves. Simmer, uncovered, without stirring, about 10 minutes or until syrup is thick. Push syrup through sieve into large heatproof bowl; cool.

Stir watermelon juice into cooled syrup; pour into 20cm x 30cm lamington pan. Cover with foil; freeze until just set. Blend or process watermelon ice with egg white until smooth, stir in extra mint, pour into 14cm x 21cm loaf pan. Cover, freeze overnight. *[Can be frozen up to 2 days.]*

Serve scoops of watermelon mint ice in glasses, with extra mint, if desired.

SERVES 4
Per serve 0.5g fat; 1.6g fibre; 703kJ (excluding extra mint).

Apple and cinnamon cakes with lemon syrup

Can be partially prepared ahead.

1/4 cup (60ml) water
1/4 cup (50g) brown sugar
1 medium (150g) unpeeled
  red apple, sliced thinly
40g low-fat margarine
1/3 cup (75g) caster sugar
1 egg, beaten lightly
1/4 cup (60ml) low-fat milk
3/4 cup (105g) self-raising flour
1/4 teaspoon ground cinnamon
1 medium (140g) lemon
1/2 cup (110g) caster sugar, extra
1/4 cup (60ml) water, extra
1 cinnamon stick

Grease four 2/3-cup (160ml) moulds. Combine the water and brown sugar in medium pan; cook, stirring, until sugar dissolves. Add apple; cook, stirring, about 10 minutes or until most of the liquid is evaporated and apples have caramelised, spoon into prepared moulds.

Beat margarine, caster sugar and egg in small bowl with electric mixer until thick and pale. Stir in milk, flour and cinnamon; pour into moulds. Bake, uncovered, in moderate oven about 20 minutes or until cooked when tested. Turn onto wire racks to cool. *[Can be made ahead to this stage. Store in an airtight container up to 1 day.]*

Using a vegetable peeler, peel a 10cm strip of rind from lemon. Combine lemon strip, 1 tablespoon lemon juice, extra sugar, extra water and cinnamon

stick in small pan; stir over heat until sugar dissolves. Simmer, uncovered, about 12 minutes or until thick and syrupy. Discard cinnamon stick and lemon rind. *[Can be made ahead to this stage. Cover; refrigerate up to 1 week. Reheat before serving.]*

Serve cakes with warm lemon syrup.

SERVES 4
Per serve 5.6g fat; 1.6g fibre; 1626kJ.

Apple and cinnamon cakes with
lemon syrup *(above)*
Petite pecan pies *(above right)*
Coffee and raspberry tortes *(right)*

Petite pecan pies

Can be prepared ahead.

8 fresh 8cm-square wonton wrappers
2 tablespoons pecans
1 egg white, beaten lightly
1 tablespoon light corn syrup
2 tablespoons brown sugar
1 teaspoon low-fat margarine, melted

Lightly grease 4 holes of 1/3-cup (80ml) muffin pan. Place 1 wrapper in each hole; top with another wrapper, ensuring corners do not cover those of first wrapper. Bake in moderate oven about 5 minutes or until crisp and browned lightly; cool.

Slice pecans into thirds lengthways, combine with remaining ingredients in small bowl; pour into wonton cases. Bake in moderately slow oven about 15 minutes or until set; cool in pans. *[Can be made 2 days ahead; store in airtight container.]*

SERVES 4

Per serve 3.7g fat; 0.7g fibre; 447kJ.

Coffee and raspberry tortes

Can be partially prepared ahead. Use fresh or frozen raspberries for this recipe. Frangelico is an Italian hazelnut-flavoured liqueur.

2 teaspoons dry instant coffee
1 cup (250ml) hot water
1/4 cup (60ml) Frangelico
8 (125g) sponge-finger biscuits
1/4 cup (60ml) low-fat sour cream
150g ricotta cheese
1/3 cup (55g) icing sugar mixture
340g fresh raspberries

Grease four 3/4-cup (180ml) ramekins. Combine coffee and water in small bowl; stir until coffee is dissolved. Stir in liqueur; cool. Cut biscuits in half crossways.

For filling, blend or process sour cream, ricotta and 1/4 cup of the icing sugar until smooth. Set aside 1/4 of the raspberries for sauce.

Place 1/2 the remaining raspberries into ramekins. Spoon 1 level tablespoon of ricotta mixture over raspberries. Dip biscuits in coffee mixture; place 2 halves in each dish. Repeat layering once more. Cover; refrigerate about 3 hours or overnight. *[Can be kept, in refrigerator, up to 2 days.]*

Blend or process remaining raspberries with remaining icing sugar until smooth. Push raspberry sauce through sieve into large bowl; discard seeds. Turn out tortes, serve with sauce.

SERVES 4

Per serve 7.9g fat; 4.7g fibre; 1012kJ.

Snacks

When you're absolutely ravenous between meals, it's very tempting to eat junk food. To help you resist, here's a great collection of delicious snacks that will pick you up without weighing you down. Some can be ready in minutes; others can be prepared ahead for those times when you know temptation is most likely to strike!

Roasted pumpkin and cumin dip

1.2kg butternut pumpkin, chopped coarsely
2 tablespoons cumin seeds
2 cloves garlic, crushed
1 tablespoon balsamic vinegar

Boil, steam or microwave pumpkin until just tender; drain.
    Combine pumpkin with cumin and garlic in baking dish; bake, uncovered, in very hot oven about 15 minutes or until pumpkin is browned lightly. Lightly mash pumpkin mixture with vinegar.

SERVES 4
Per serve 1.9g fat; 4.3g fibre; 477kJ.

Hummus

1 tablespoon lemon juice
1/2 small (40g) brown onion, chopped finely
1 clove garlic, crushed
1/2 teaspoon ground cumin
1/2 x 425g can chickpeas, rinsed, drained
1/4 cup (60ml) low-fat milk
1 teaspoon smooth peanut butter
1/4 teaspoon sesame oil
2 teaspoons chopped fresh coriander leaves

Heat lemon juice in small pan; add onion and garlic. Cook, stirring, until onion softens. Blend or process onion mixture with remaining ingredients until smooth.

SERVES 4
Per serve 3g fat; 5g fibre; 474kJ.

Quick beetroot dip

225g can sliced beetroot, drained
1/4 cup (60ml) yogurt
1 teaspoon ground coriander
2 teaspoons ground cumin

Blend or process all ingredients until smooth.

SERVES 4
Per serve 0.8g fat; 1.5g fibre; 136kJ.

Bagel chips

Use plain, wholemeal, soy-and-linseed or any savoury bagel of your choice for this recipe.

2 savoury bagels
cooking-oil spray
1 clove garlic, halved
2 tablespoons tandoori paste
2 tablespoons horseradish cream

Cut bagels into paper-thin rounds; place rounds, in single layer, on oven trays. Coat rounds with cooking-oil spray; rub cut edge of garlic over rounds. Using pastry brush, spread half of the rounds with tandoori paste, then spread remaining rounds with horseradish cream. Bake, uncovered, in moderate oven about 10 minutes or until browned lightly and crisp.

SERVES 4
Per serve 4.7g fat; 1.9g fibre; 745kJ.

Roasted pumpkin and cumin dip *(centre)*
Hummus *(right)*
Quick beetroot dip *(back)*
Bagel chips *(front)*

Corn bread with roast beef, rocket and horseradish cream

4 thick slices corn bread
1/4 cup (60ml) low-fat sour cream
2 teaspoons horseradish relish
200g shaved rare roast beef
50g baby rocket leaves

Cut each slice of bread into 4 pieces. Combine sour cream and relish in small bowl; mix well. Top bread with roast beef and rocket; drizzle with horseradish cream.

SERVES 4

Per serve 14.4g fat; 4.2g fibre; 1188kJ.

Spinach and fetta pide

2 tablespoons lemon juice
1 medium (150g) brown onion, sliced thinly
2 cloves garlic, crushed
100g baby spinach leaves
2 small pide
1 hard-boiled egg, grated finely
60g low-fat fetta, crumbled

Heat juice in medium pan; cook onion and garlic, stirring, until onion softens. Stir in spinach; cook, stirring, until spinach is just wilted.

Cut a 5cm-wide x 4cm-deep wedge from top of each pide. Trim bread from under lids; reserve lids. Place pide on oven tray; fill with spinach mixture, pressing in firmly. Sprinkle egg and fetta over spinach; replace lids. Bake, uncovered, in hot oven about 10 minutes or until bread is crisp. Cut into thick slices; serve with lemon wedges, if desired.

SERVES 4

Per serve 4.4g fat; 3.9g fibre; 1198kJ (excluding lemon wedges).

Lamb pide

2 small (160g) brown onions, chopped finely
2 cloves garlic, crushed
250g minced lamb
1 tablespoon tomato paste
1/4 teaspoon hot paprika
1 teaspoon ground cumin
2 small pide
1/4 cup (25g) finely grated low-fat mozzarella cheese
2 tablespoons finely chopped fresh mint leaves

Heat oiled medium pan; cook onion and garlic, stirring, until onion softens. Add lamb, paste, paprika and cumin; cook, stirring, until lamb is cooked through.

Split bread, place bases on oven tray, spread with lamb mixture, sprinkle with cheese and mint; replace tops. Bake, uncovered, in hot oven about 10 minutes or until bread is crisp. Cut into thick slices; serve with lemon wedges, if desired.

SERVES 4

Per serve 8.6g fat; 3.9g fibre; 1549kJ (excluding lemon wedges).

Oven-dried corn tortilla chips

Can be prepared ahead.

8 corn tortillas
cooking-oil spray
2 teaspoons Cajun seasoning

Coat one side of one tortilla with cooking-oil spray, sprinkle with seasoning, cut into quarters. Place on oven tray in single layer; bake, uncovered, in moderately slow oven about 15 minutes or until crisp. If desired, place tortilla quarters over the handle of a wooden spoon to shape. Repeat with remaining tortillas, spray and seasoning. *[Can be made 2 days ahead; keep in an airtight container.]*

SERVES 4

Per serve 6.9g fat; 2.2g fibre; 785kJ.

Corn bread with roast beef, rocket and horseradish cream *(above left)*
Spinach and fetta pide *(left)*
Lamb pide *(far left)*

Herb and garlic toasts

1 long French bread stick
cooking-oil spray
1 clove garlic, halved
1/4 cup finely chopped fresh parsley
1/4 cup finely chopped fresh chives
1/4 cup finely chopped fresh basil leaves

Cut bread into 2cm-wide diagonal slices; place, in single layer, on oven tray. Coat tops with cooking-oil spray, rub with cut surface of garlic; sprinkle with combined herbs. Bake, uncovered, in moderate oven about 7 minutes or until browned lightly.

SERVES 4

Per serve 3.3g fat; 2.3g fibre; 696kJ.

Spicy tomato dip

425g can tomatoes
2 cloves garlic, crushed
1 small (80g) brown onion, sliced thinly
1 teaspoon Cajun seasoning

Combine undrained crushed tomatoes with remaining ingredients in small pan; cook, stirring, until onion is soft and sauce has thickened.

SERVES 4

Per serve 0.4g fat; 2g fibre; 116kJ.

Mediterranean ciabatta

3 medium (600g) red capsicums
4 small (360g) zucchini, sliced thinly lengthways
2 large (500g) tomatoes, sliced thickly
cooking-oil spray
4 x 2cm-thick slices ciabatta
1/4 cup (60ml) baba ghanoush
1 tablespoon sun-dried tomato pesto
1 tablespoon fresh basil leaves

Quarter capsicums, remove and discard seeds and membranes. Roast under grill or in very hot oven, skin-side up, until skin blisters and blackens. Cover capsicum pieces in plastic or paper for 5 minutes, peel away skin.

Lightly coat zucchini and tomato with cooking-oil spray; cook, in batches, on heated griddle (or grill or barbecue) until browned both sides and just tender.

Toast ciabatta both sides; top with baba ghanoush, pesto, tomato, capsicum, zucchini and basil.

SERVES 4

Per serve 2.8g fat; 5.1g fibre; 792kJ.

Baba ghanoush

Can be prepared ahead.

2 small (460g) eggplants, peeled, chopped coarsely
1/3 cup (80ml) yogurt
1 tablespoon lemon juice
2 cloves garlic, crushed
1 teaspoon peanut butter
1 teaspoon ground cumin
1/2 teaspoon sesame oil
2 tablespoons finely chopped fresh coriander leaves

Place eggplant, in a single layer, in baking dish. Bake in moderately hot oven about 40 minutes or until tender. Blend or process eggplant with remaining ingredients until smooth. Cover; refrigerate about 30 minutes or until cool. *[Can be made a day ahead. Cover; refrigerate overnight.]*

SERVES 4

Per serve 2.3g fat; 3.2g fibre; 212kJ.

Oven-dried corn tortilla crisps *(below right)*
Herb and garlic toasts *(below left)*
Spicy tomato dip *(below centre)*
Mediterranean ciabatta *(below back)*
Baba ghanoush *(below front)*

China spoons from Accoutrement

Potato wedges with two sauces (left)
Baked lemon-thyme ricotta with sourdough (back right)
Polenta triangles with smoked salmon (front right)

Potato wedges with two sauces

6 large (1.8kg) potatoes
2 egg whites, beaten lightly
2 tablespoons garlic salt

SWEET CHILLI DIPPING SAUCE
1/2 small (75g) red capsicum
3 birdseye chillies, seeded, chopped finely
1/2 cup (125ml) water
2 cloves garlic, crushed
1 cup (220g) sugar
2 teaspoons balsamic vinegar

LIME GUACAMOLE
1 small (200g) avocado, chopped coarsely
1/2 teaspoon finely grated lime rind
1 tablespoon lime juice
1 small (100g) red onion, chopped finely
1 medium (190g) tomato, seeded, chopped finely

Boil, steam or microwave unpeeled potatoes until just tender; drain. Cut potatoes into wedges; combine in large bowl with egg white and garlic salt. Place potato, in single layer, on oiled oven trays; bake, uncovered, in very hot oven about 30 minutes or until lightly browned and crisp. Serve with Sweet chilli dipping sauce and Lime guacamole.

Sweet chilli dipping sauce Halve capsicum, remove and discard seeds and membranes. Roast under grill or in very hot oven, skin-side up, until skin blisters and blackens. Cover capsicum pieces in plastic or paper for 5 minutes, peel away skin; chop capsicum coarsely.

Blend or process capsicum with chilli, water and garlic until smooth. Combine capsicum mixture with sugar and vinegar in medium pan; cook, stirring, until sugar dissolves. Simmer, uncovered, about 25 minutes or until sauce is thick and syrupy. [Can be made 1 week ahead; store in refrigerator.]

Lime guacamole Combine all ingredients in medium bowl; mix well.

SERVES 4
Per serve 9.2g fat; 10.5g fibre; 2592kJ.

Baked lemon-thyme ricotta with sourdough

Baked lemon-thyme ricotta has to be made ahead. For best results, make the day before required. We used wholemeal sourdough, but any French stick could be used instead.

1 cup (200g) low-fat ricotta cheese
1¼ cups (250g) low-fat cottage cheese
1 egg, beaten lightly
1 clove garlic, crushed
1 tablespoon finely chopped fresh lemon thyme
2 tablespoons coarsely chopped seeded black olives
8 thin slices sourdough

Whisk ricotta in small bowl until smooth. Stir in cottage cheese, egg, garlic and half of the lemon thyme. Spoon mixture into oiled 2-cup (500ml) ovenproof dish, sprinkle with olives. Bake, covered, in moderate oven 35 minutes. Uncover, bake further 20 minutes or until just set. Sprinkle with remaining lemon thyme; cool.

Cover, refrigerate several hours until firm; drain off excess liquid. [Should be made a day ahead.]

Just before serving, toast bread, cut diagonally, serve with baked ricotta.

SERVES 4
Per serve 6.6g fat; 1.3g fibre; 925kJ.

Polenta triangles with smoked salmon

Can be partially prepared ahead. The polenta mixture needs to be refrigerated at least 1 hour before cutting into triangles and cooking.

2 cloves garlic, crushed
1 large (200g) brown onion, chopped finely
4 medium (800g) potatoes
2 cups (500ml) chicken stock
1/2 cup (85g) polenta
100g sliced smoked salmon
2 teaspoons finely grated lime rind
200ml goat milk yogurt
2 teaspoons finely chopped fresh dill

Heat oiled small pan; cook garlic and onion, stirring, until onion softens.

Boil, steam or microwave potatoes until just tender; drain. Mash potatoes.

Bring stock to boil in medium pan, gradually add polenta; simmer, stirring, about 10 minutes or until soft and thick. Stir in onion mixture and potato. Spread mixture into oiled 15cm-square cake pan; cool. Cover polenta; refrigerate until firm. [Can be made a day ahead.]

Remove polenta from pan; cut polenta in half to form two 7.5cm x 15cm rectangles. Cut each rectangle to give six 2.5cm-wide x 7.5cm-long x 5.5cm-deep fingers. Turn fingers so 5.5cm side is facing; cut in half diagonally to form 2 triangles (24 triangles in all).

Heat oiled large pan; cook polenta triangles, in batches, until golden brown all over and heated through. Cut salmon to fit triangles. Top polenta triangles with salmon and combined rind, yogurt and dill.

MAKES 24
Per triangle 0.6g fat; 0.8g fibre; 201kJ.

Beef empanadas

Can be partially prepared ahead. We used canned pinto beans with chilli sauce for this recipe.

1³/₄ cups (260g) plain flour
60g quark cheese
¹/₂ cup (125ml) warm
**   water, approximately**
250g minced beef
1 teaspoon ground cumin
¹/₂ x 425g can Mexican-style
**   chilli beans**
1 tablespoon finely chopped
**   fresh oregano**

Blend or process flour and cheese until combined; add enough water to make a soft, sticky dough. Turn dough onto floured surface; knead until smooth. Wrap in plastic wrap; stand 30 minutes. *[Can be made 1 day ahead; refrigerate until required.]*

Meanwhile, for filling, cook beef and cumin in heated medium pan until browned. Add beans; cook until mixture is heated through. Stir in oregano; cool.

Roll out dough on floured surface until 2mm thick. Cut 8.5cm rounds from pastry and re-rolled scraps. You will get approximately 24 rounds.

Place 1 level tablespoon of filling in centre of each round, fold round in half to enclose filling; pinch edges to seal. Cover tightly with plastic wrap; refrigerate 15 minutes. *[Can be made up to 3 hours ahead.]*

Place empanadas on baking-paper-lined oven trays; bake, uncovered, in moderately hot oven about 15 minutes or until brown and crisp.

SERVES 4

Per serve 8.2g fat; 4.5g fibre; 1522kJ.

Bread samosas

Can be partially prepared ahead.

1 large (300g) potato, chopped finely
5 green onions, sliced thinly
1 tablespoon mild curry powder
300g can chickpeas, rinsed, drained
¹/₂ cup (60g) frozen peas, thawed
1 tablespoon tomato paste
¹/₄ cup (60ml) water
24 slices white bread
cooking-oil spray

Heat oiled medium pan, cook potato and onion, stirring, until onion is soft. Add curry powder, cook, stirring, until fragrant. Add chickpeas, peas, paste and water, cook, uncovered, until potato is tender, stirring occasionally; cool. *[Can be made 1 day ahead; cover, refrigerate until required.]*

Cut bread into 10cm rounds. Place 1 tablespoon of potato mixture on each round, brush edges with a little water, fold rounds in half to enclose filling; press edges together with a fork. Place samosas on greased oven trays; coat with cooking-oil spray. Bake, uncovered, in moderate oven about 20 minutes or until brown and crisp.

MAKES 24

Per samosa 0.8g fat; 1.3g fibre; 246kJ.

Tandoori chicken bites

Soak bamboo skewers in water for at least 1 hour before using to prevent them burning.

500g chicken breast fillets
2 tablespoons tandoori paste
1 cup (250ml) low-fat yogurt
1 teaspoon ground cumin
1 teaspoon ground coriander
1 (130g) Lebanese cucumber, seeded,
**   chopped finely**
1 tablespoon lemon juice
1 tablespoon finely chopped fresh
**   coriander leaves**

Cut chicken into bite-size pieces; combine with paste, ¹/₂ cup (125ml) of the yogurt, half the cumin and half the ground coriander in medium bowl. Cover; refrigerate 3 hours or overnight.

Thread chicken onto skewers; cook, in batches, on heated oiled griddle (or grill or barbecue) until browned all over and cooked through.

Meanwhile, combine remaining yogurt with remaining cumin and ground coriander, cucumber, juice and fresh coriander in small bowl; mix well.

Serve Tandoori chicken bites with yogurt mixture.

SERVES 8

Per serve 2.1g fat; 0.4g fibre; 420kJ.

Beef empanadas *(back left)*
Bread samosas *(centre left)*
Tandoori chicken bites *(front left)*
Chilli prawn and mango cups *(above right)*
Vegetable rolls with dipping sauce *(right)*

Chilli prawn and mango cups

3 sheets fillo pastry
cooking-oil spray
200g shelled small cooked prawns,
     chopped finely
1 small (300g) mango, chopped finely
1/2 small (50g) red onion,
     chopped finely
1 birdseye chilli, seeded,
     chopped finely
2 tablespoons finely chopped
     fresh chives

Cut fillo into 4cm squares. Layer
4 squares together, spraying with oil
between each layer and ensuring corners
do not cover those of previous square,
to make 1 stack. Repeat with remaining
squares to make 52 stacks.
    Press 12 stacks into oiled 12-hole
small (2 tablespoon/40ml) muffin pan.
Bake in moderate oven 5 minutes or until
browned. Repeat with remaining stacks.
    Combine prawns, mango, onion,
chilli and chives in small bowl; spoon
rounded teaspoons of mixture into
pastry cases.

MAKES 52

Per cup 0.3g fat; 0.1g fibre; 48kJ.

Vegetable rolls with dipping sauce

1 large (180g) carrot
2 (260g) Lebanese cucumbers, seeded
2 medium (400g) red capsicums, seeded
1/3 cup (80ml) lime juice
2 tablespoons chopped fresh
     coriander leaves
12 x 21cm-round rice paper sheets
1/2 cup (100g) firmly packed
     brown sugar
1/4 cup (60ml) water
1/4 cup (60ml) sweet chilli sauce

Cut carrot, cucumber and capsicum into
thin 4cm-long strips; combine with
1 tablespoon of the lime juice and
2 teaspoons of the coriander in medium
bowl, divide into 12 portions.
    Place 1 sheet rice paper in large
heatproof bowl of hot water, soak about
1 minute or until softened; gently lift
from water, place on board. Place
1 portion vegetable mixture across lower
edge of rice paper; fold in sides, roll to
enclose filling. Repeat with remaining
rice paper sheets and vegetable mixture.
    Place remaining juice, sugar, water
and sauce in small pan; stir over heat,
without boiling, until sugar is dissolved.
Simmer, uncovered, without stirring,
about 5 minutes or until mixture thickens;
cool. Stir in remaining coriander; serve.

SERVES 4

Per serve 0.8g fat; 4.4g fibre; 900kJ.

Breakfast and drinks

If you're bored with the same old toast-and-grapefruit breakfast, get your day off to a new start with something a little different. From yummy dishes you can whip up in a trice for a leisurely weekend brunch, to refreshing fruit drinks you can sip as you head for the door, all the recipes in this chapter combine delicious flavours with a fresh, low-fat approach.

Eggs with asparagus, grilled ham and onion jam

We used 48g eggs for this recipe.

2 medium (340g) red onions, sliced thinly
2 tablespoons balsamic vinegar
1/3 cup (75g) firmly packed brown sugar
2 tablespoons chicken stock
100g shaved leg ham
500g asparagus, trimmed
4 eggs

Heat medium oiled pan; cook onion, stirring, until almost soft. Stir in vinegar and sugar; cook, stirring, until sugar dissolves. Stir in stock; simmer, uncovered, about 15 minutes or until onion caramelises, cool.

Place ham, in single layer, on oven tray; grill until browned lightly.

Boil, steam or microwave asparagus until just tender; drain.

Heat oiled large pan; fry eggs until cooked as desired. Serve eggs with asparagus, ham and onion jam.

SERVES 4

Per serve 6.3g fat; 2.6g fibre; 868kJ.

Swiss muesli with grilled mangoes and blueberries

1 1/2 cups (135g) traditional rolled oats
1 cup (250ml) low-fat milk
300ml low-fat yogurt with honey
2 medium (860g) mangoes
1 medium (150g) apple, chopped finely
2 tablespoons lemon juice
100g fresh blueberries
2 tablespoons honey

Combine oats, half the milk and half the yogurt in large bowl; cover, refrigerate 20 minutes.

Meanwhile, cut through mangoes on both sides of seed; scoop out flesh with a spoon. Cut mango halves into thick slices. Cook mango on heated griddle (or grill or barbecue) until browned both sides.

Stir remaining milk, remaining yogurt, apple and juice into oat mixture. Top with blueberries and grilled mango, drizzle with honey.

SERVES 4

Per serve 4.3g fat; 5.7g fibre; 1530kJ.

Gazpacho juice

850ml can tomato juice
1 small (100g) red onion, chopped
1 small (130g) green cucumber, peeled, chopped
1 birdseye chilli, seeded, chopped
1 tablespoon Worcestershire sauce
1/4 cup (60ml) lime juice
4 untrimmed (600g) celery sticks

Blend or process tomato juice, onion, cucumber, chilli, sauce and lime juice until smooth. Divide between four glasses; garnish with celery.

SERVES 4

Per serve 0.2g fat; 2.7g fibre; 285kJ.

Eggs with asparagus, grilled ham and onion jam *(far right)*
Swiss muesli with grilled mangoes and blueberries *(back)*
Gazpacho juice *(front)*

Pancakes with spiced bananas

1 cup (220g) sugar
10 cloves
2 tablespoons dark rum
1/2 cup (125ml) water
1 cup (150g) self-raising flour
1 cup (250ml) buttermilk
2 egg whites
2 large (460g) bananas,
 sliced diagonally

Combine sugar, cloves, rum and water in small pan; stir over heat, without boiling, until sugar dissolves. Bring to boil; simmer, uncovered, about 5 minutes or until syrup is slightly thickened.

Meanwhile, combine flour, milk and egg whites in large bowl; whisk until batter is smooth. Heat oiled large pan. Pour in 2 tablespoons batter for each pancake; cook until browned lightly both sides. Repeat with remaining batter.

Place bananas, in single layer, on oiled oven tray, brush with 2 tablespoons syrup; reserve remaining syrup. Grill bananas until just soft and browned.

For each serving, place 1 pancake on serving plate, top with 1/8 of the banana mixture, another pancake, another 1/8 of the banana mixture, then another pancake. Drizzle with reserved syrup.

SERVES 4

Per serve 1.8g fat; 3.1g fibre; 2136kJ.

Porridge with sticky fruits

1 cup (150g) dried apricots
2 tablespoons honey
1 cup (250ml) water
1 cinnamon stick
1 tablespoon finely grated lemon rind
1 cup (230g) fresh dates
2 1/4 cups (200g) traditional
 rolled oats
6 cups (1.5 litres) low-fat milk
1 tablespoon flaked almonds, toasted

Combine apricots, honey, water, cinnamon and rind in small pan; bring to boil. Simmer, uncovered, about 5 minutes or until syrup has thickened slightly; cool. Cut dates in half lengthways, discard seeds; add dates to apricot mixture.

Combine oats and milk in medium pan; cook, stirring, about 10 minutes or until mixture thickens.

Drain fruit over large bowl; reserve syrup. Spoon porridge into bowls; top with apricots, dates and nuts, drizzle with syrup.

SERVES 4

Per serve 5.6g fat; 21.5g fibre; 2496kJ.

Mango buttermilk booster

**1 large (600g) mango,
chopped coarsely**
1 cup (250ml) buttermilk
1 cup (250ml) low-fat milk
2 tablespoons low-fat milk powder
4 ice-cubes
1 scoop (50g) low-fat ice-cream

Blend or process all ingredients
until smooth.

SERVES 2
Per serve 4.8g fat; 3.2g fibre; 1448kJ.

Fruit cup crush

2 large (1.2kg) mangoes
1/2 medium (1.3kg) rockmelon
1 medium (1.25kg) pineapple
2 cups (500ml) orange juice
2 tablespoons caster sugar

Cut peeled fruit into medium pieces.
Blend or process fruit, in batches, until
smooth. Stir in orange juice and sugar.

SERVES 4 (Makes about 1.5 litres)
Per serve 1.4g fat; 12.4g fibre; 1681kJ.

Mixed fruit and yogurt drink

*You will need about 3 passionfruit for
this recipe.*

1/2 small (400g) pawpaw
1 large (300g) orange
2 medium (170g) kiwi fruit
1/2 small (400g) pineapple
1/2 cup (75g) blueberries
150g raspberries
**1/4 cup (60ml) fresh
passionfruit pulp**
1/2 cup (125ml) yogurt

Peel pawpaw, orange, kiwi fruit and
pineapple; cut fruit into medium
pieces. Blend or process fruit
and remaining ingredients,
in batches, until smooth.

SERVES 8 (Makes about 2 litres)
Per serve 0.8g fat;
4.5g fibre; 265kJ.

Fruit cup crush; mixed fruit and yogurt drink;
mango buttermilk booster *(front to back)*

Pancakes with spiced bananas *(top left)*
Porridge with sticky fruits *(far left)*

French fruit toast with maple yogurt

1 egg white
1/2 cup (125ml) low-fat milk
6 slices fruit loaf
200ml low-fat vanilla yogurt
1 tablespoon maple syrup

Whisk egg white and milk in large bowl until combined. Cut bread in half diagonally. Heat oiled large pan; dip each piece of bread into milk mixture. Cook, in batches, until browned lightly both sides. To serve, place 3 pieces of toast on each plate, top with combined yogurt and syrup. Serve with fresh berries, if desired.

SERVES 4

Per serve 2g fat; 1.3g fibre; 768kJ (excluding berries).

Ham, avocado and roasted tomato toast

4 large (360g) egg tomatoes
1 tablespoon brown sugar
1 small (100g) red onion, sliced thinly
150g shaved leg ham
4 thick slices vienna loaf
1/2 small (100g) avocado, sliced thinly
1 tablespoon shredded fresh
    basil leaves

Cut tomatoes in half lengthways; place cut-side up on oiled oven tray, sprinkle with sugar. Bake tomato, uncovered, in very hot oven 15 minutes. Add onion; bake further 15 minutes or until tomato is soft.

Cook ham in heated small pan until browned lightly and almost crisp. Toast bread; top with ham, onion, tomato, avocado and basil.

SERVES 4

Per serve 5.9g fat; 2.6g fibre; 652kJ.

French fruit toast with maple yogurt *(above left)*
Ham, avocado and roasted tomato toast *(left)*
Low-fat toasted muesli *(above right)*
Bagels with scrambled eggs and
smoked salmon *(above right, centre)*
Quick banana bread *(above far right)*

Low-fat toasted muesli

We used a cereal called All-Bran.

2 cups (180g) traditional rolled oats
1/2 cup (35g) bran cereal
1/2 cup (125ml) honey
1/2 cup (125ml) fresh orange juice
**1/2 cup (75g) coarsely chopped
   dried apricots**
**1/2 cup (45g) coarsely chopped
   dried apples**
1/2 cup (85g) raisins
1/4 cup (35g) dried currants
3 cups (60g) puffed rice

Combine oats and bran in large bowl.
   Heat honey and orange juice in small pan, stirring until honey is melted. Add half of the honey mixture to oat mixture; mix well. Spread mixture over baking-paper-lined oven tray; bake, uncovered, in moderately slow oven about 20 minutes or until browned lightly, stirring every 5 minutes.
   Return mixture to same large bowl, add remaining ingredients and remaining honey mixture; spread over 2 baking-paper-lined oven trays. Bake, uncovered, in moderately slow oven about 10 minutes or until browned

lightly, stirring midway through cooking time; cool. Store in an airtight container up to 2 weeks.
MAKES 8 CUPS
Per cup 2.6g fat; 4.6g fibre; 1092kJ.

Bagels with scrambled eggs and smoked salmon

2 eggs, beaten lightly
10 egg whites
**2 tablespoons finely chopped
   fresh chives**
2 bagels
**1 small (130g) green cucumber,
   sliced thinly**
200g sliced smoked salmon

Whisk eggs, whites and chives together in medium bowl. Heat oiled medium pan, add egg mixture, gently stir over low heat until almost set.
   Split bagels in half; toast both sides. Top bagel halves with cucumber, eggs and salmon.
SERVES 4
Per serve 7g fat; 2.1g fibre; 1217kJ.

Quick banana bread

*You will need 1 large overripe banana
for this recipe.*

1 1/4 cups (185g) self-raising flour
1 teaspoon ground cinnamon
1 tablespoon low-fat margarine
1/2 cup (110g) sugar
1 egg, beaten lightly
1/4 cup (60ml) low-fat milk
1/2 cup mashed banana

Line base and sides of 14cm x 21cm loaf pan with baking paper.
   Combine flour and cinnamon in large bowl; rub in margarine. Stir in sugar, egg, milk and banana; do not overmix, batter should be lumpy. Spoon mixture into prepared pan; bake in hot oven about 20 minutes or until cooked when tested.
SERVES 4
Per serve 4g fat; 2.8g fibre; 1389kJ.

GLOSSARY

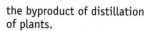

cottage cheese
ricotta
quark
goat cheese
fetta
mozzarella
parmesan
cheddar

ALCOHOL AND LIQUEURS
Cointreau an orange-flavoured liqueur.
Frangelico a hazelnut-flavoured liqueur.
Grand Marnier an orange-flavoured liqueur.
Rum, dark we prefer to use an underproof rum.
Tia Maria a coffee-flavoured liqueur.

ANGOSTURA AROMATIC BITTERS
Angostura is a brand of bitters, based on rum, infused with aromatic bark, herbs and spices.

BABA GHANOUSH
Dip based on eggplant, tahini, garlic and salt.

BACON RASHERS
Also known as bacon slices.

BAGEL
Small, ring-shaped bread roll, boiled in water then baked.

BEAN SPROUTS
Also known as bean shoots. New growths of beans and seeds, such as mung bean, soy bean, alfalfa and snow pea sprouts.

BEEF AND VEAL
Beef eye fillet tenderloin.
Beef rump steak boneless tender cut.
Veal cutlets choice chop from the mid-loin (back) area.
Veal leg steaks best cut to have pounded into schnitzels or scaloppine.

BREADCRUMBS
Packaged fine-textured, purchased white breadcrumbs.
Stale 1- or 2-day-old bread made into crumbs by blending or processing.

CAJUN SEASONING
This packaged mix of herbs and spices can include paprika, basil, onion, fennel, thyme, cayenne and white pepper.

CAPERS
The grey-green buds of a warm-climate shrub. The buds are sold pickled, or dried and salted. Their piquancy adds to dressings and sauces.

CAPSICUM
Also known as bell pepper. Discard seeds and membranes before use.

CARAWAY
Available in seed or ground form; used in sweet and savoury dishes.

CARDAMOM
Can be bought in pod, seed or ground form. Has a distinctive, aromatic, sweetly rich flavour.

CHEESE
Cheddar cheese, low-fat we used one with a fat content of not more than 7%.
Cottage cheese we used one with 2g fat per 100g.
Fetta cheese, low-fat we used a fetta with an average fat content of 15%.
Goat cheese made from goat milk. Has an earthy, strong taste and is available in both soft and firm textures.
Mozzarella, low-fat we used one with 17.5g fat per 100g.
Parmesan a sharp-tasting, dry, hard cheese, made from skim or part-skim milk and aged for at least a year.
Quark a soft, mildly sour cheese made from skim milk with 9.5g fat per 100g.
Ricotta, low-fat a fresh, unripened cheese made from whey with 8.5g fat per 100g.

CHICKEN
Chicken mince also known as ground chicken.
Chicken tenderloin thin strip of meat under the breast.
Chicken thigh cutlets thigh with skin and bone intact; also known as chicken chop.

CHICKPEAS
Round sandy-coloured legumes, also known as garbanzos, hummus or channa.

CHILLI POWDER
Made from ground chillies, it can be used as a substitute for fresh chillies in the proportion of 1/2 teaspoon ground chilli powder to 1 medium chopped fresh chilli.

CHILLIES
Also known as hot peppers or chiles; available in many types and sizes. Generally, the smaller the chilli the hotter it is. Use rubber gloves when seeding and chopping fresh chillies as they can burn your skin. Removing membranes and seeds reduces the heat level.

CHINESE CABBAGE
Also known as Peking cabbage or wong bok.

CHOY SUM
Also known as flowering bok choy or flowering white cabbage.

CIABATTA
Italian crusty wood-fired bread.

COOKING-OIL SPRAY
We used a cholesterol-free non-stick cooking spray made from canola oil.

CORIANDER
Also known as cilantro or Chinese parsley. Bright-green-leafed herb with a pungent flavour.

CORNFLOUR
Also known as cornstarch; used as a thickening agent in cooking.

CORN SYRUP
Available in light or dark colour; either can be substituted for the other. Glucose syrup (liquid glucose) can be substituted.

COUSCOUS
A fine grain-like cereal product, made from semolina.

CUSTARD POWDER
Packaged, vanilla pudding mixture.

DEHYDRATED SUN-DRIED TOMATOES
Available loose (by weight) or in packets (not packed in oil).

EGGPLANT
Also known as aubergine.

ESSENCES
Also known as extracts; generally the byproduct of distillation of plants.

FILLO PASTRY
Also known as phyllo. Chilled or frozen purchased tissue-thin pastry sheets that are very versatile, lending themselves to both sweet and savoury dishes.

FISH FILLETS
Fish pieces that have been boned and skinned.

FLOUR
Plain all-purpose flour.
Self-raising plain flour sifted with baking powder (a raising agent consisting mainly of 2 parts cream of tartar to 1 part bicarbonate of soda) in the proportion of 1 cup flour to 2 level teaspoons baking powder.

FRENCH DRESSING
Use any oil-free or fat-free variety.

FRUCHE
Commercial dessert with less than 0.5g fat per 100g. Similar to fromage frais.

GELATINE (gelatin) We used powdered gelatine.

GHEE Clarified butter; with the milk solids removed, this fat can be heated to high temperature without burning.

GINGER, FRESH also known as green or root ginger. The thick, gnarled root of a tropical plant.

GOAT MILK YOGURT Available from health food stores.

GREEN PEPPERCORNS Unripe berry of the pepper plant usually sold packed in brine.

HAZELNUTS Also known as filberts. Rich, sweet nut with a brown inedible skin that is removed by rubbing heated nuts in a tea towel.

HERBS We have specified when to use fresh and dried herbs. We used dried (not ground) herbs in the ratio of 1:4 for fresh herbs.

HORSERADISH
Cream a creamy prepared paste of grated horseradish, vinegar, oil and sugar.
Fresh a plant of the mustard family; the root has a hot, pungent flavour and is often used as a condiment.

ITALIAN DRESSING Use an oil-free or fat-free variety.

KAFFIR LIME
Fruit medium-sized citrus fruit with wrinkly yellow-green skin, used in Thai cooking.
Leaves aromatic leaves used fresh or dried in Asian dishes.

KETJAP MANIS Indonesian sweet, thick soy sauce which has sugar and spices added.

KITCHEN STRING String constructed of an untreated natural material specifically for use in cooking; synthetic string will melt in the oven.

KIWI FRUIT Also known as Chinese gooseberry.

KUMARA Polynesian name of orange-fleshed sweet potato often confused with yam.

LAMB
Eye of loin a cut from a row of loin chops, with the bone and fat removed.
Fillet tenderloin; small piece of meat from row of loin chops or cutlets.
Lamb mince also known as ground lamb.

LAVASH Flat sheets of unleavened bread.

LEBANESE CUCUMBER Long and thin-skinned. Also known as the European or burpless cucumber.

LEMON GRASS A sharp-edged grass, smelling and tasting of lemon. The white lower part of each stem is used.

LEMON PEPPER SEASONING A blend of crushed black peppercorns, lemon, herbs and spices.

LENTILS Many varieties of dried legumes, identified by and named after their colour.

LOW-FAT ICE-CREAM We used an ice-cream with 3% fat.

LOW-FAT MARGARINE We used polyunsaturated spread, containing 2g of fat per 5g.

LOW-FAT MAYONNAISE We used cholesterol-free mayonnaise with 3g fat per 100g.

LOW-FAT MILK We used milk with 1.4g fat per 100ml.

LOW-FAT SOUR CREAM We used light sour cream with 18.5g fat per 100g.

LOW-FAT THICKENED CREAM We used thickened cream with 18g fat per 100ml.

LOW-FAT YOGURT We used yogurt with a fat content of less than 0.2%.

MAPLE-FLAVOURED SYRUP Also known as pancake syrup. Made from cane sugar and artificial maple flavouring; is not the same as maple syrup.

MAPLE SYRUP Distilled sap of the maple tree.

MESCLUN Often sold as mixed small leaves for salad, and consists of an assortment of edible greens and flowers.

MEXICAN CHILLI POWDER A blend of chilli, cumin, oregano, garlic and salt.

MILK
Buttermilk cultured milk with 1.8g fat per 100ml and a slightly sour taste. Low-fat yogurt can be substituted.
Evaporated, low-fat we used canned milk with 1.6g fat per 100ml.
Low-fat we used low-fat milk with 1.4g fat per 100ml.

Skim we used skim milk with 0.1g fat per 100ml.

MINCE MEAT Also known as ground meat, as in beef, pork, lamb and veal.

MIRIN A sweet low-alcohol rice wine used in Japanese cooking.

MIZUNA Feathery green salad leaf with a sharp flavour.

MUSHROOMS
Button small, cultivated white mushrooms with a delicate, subtle flavour.
Shiitake cultivated fresh mushroom; has a rich, meaty flavour.
Swiss brown light to dark brown mushrooms with mild, earthy flavour.

MUSTARD
Black mustard seeds also known as brown mustard seeds. More pungent than the white (or yellow) seeds used in most mustards.
Dijon a pale brown, fairly mild French mustard.
Seeded also known as wholegrain. A flavourful coarse-grain mustard made from crushed mustard seeds.

NAAN An Indian flat bread, slightly leavened with yeast.

NASHI Also called Japanese or Asian pear; similar in appearance to an apple.

NOODLES
Bean thread noodles also known as cellophane or glass noodles, or bean thread vermicelli.
Fresh egg noodles made from wheat flour and eggs; strands vary in thickness.
Ramen a crinkly or straight dried wheat noodle.
Soba a buckwheat noodle. Comes in varying proportions of buckwheat and wheat flour; the colour varies accordingly, from brownish through to almost white.

OIL
Extra virgin olive oil the highest quality olive oil, obtained from the first pressing of the olives.
Olive mono-unsaturated. Made from the pressing of tree-ripened olives. Good for everyday cooking and as a salad-dressing ingredient.

Fresh herbs

1. Lemon thyme
2. Sage
3. Marjoram
4. Rosemary
5. Curly parsley
6. Flat-leaf parsley
7. Coriander
8. Dill
9. Tarragon
10. Thyme
11. Chives
12. Mint
13. Basil

rockmelon

pawpaw

nashi pear

kiwi fruit

Peanut pressed from ground peanuts. The most commonly used oil in stir-frying because of its high smoke point.
Sesame made from roasted, crushed, white sesame seeds; used as a flavouring.
Vegetable any of a number of oils having a plant rather than an animal source.

ONION
Brown and white are interchangeable. Their pungent flesh adds flavour to a vast range of dishes.
Green also known as scallion or (incorrectly) shallot. An immature onion picked before the bulb has formed, having a bright-green edible stalk.
Red also known as Spanish, red Spanish or Bermuda onion. A sweet flavoured, large, purple-red onion; good eaten raw in salads.

PANCETTA An Italian salt-cured pork roll, usually cut from the belly. Bacon can be substituted in most recipes.

PAPRIKA Ground dried red capsicum (bell pepper), available sweet or hot.

PARSLEY, FLAT-LEAF Also known as continental parsley or Italian parsley.

PASSIONFRUIT Also known as granadilla. A small tropical fruit, native to Brazil, with edible black seeds.

PASTA
Fettuccine ribbon pasta averaging 5mm in width, made from durum wheat semolina and egg, available fresh or dried, plain or flavoured with various herbs, pepper or vegetable essences.

Gnocchi Italian "dumplings" made of potatoes, semolina or flour; cooked in boiling water or baked with a sauce.
Lasagne available as fresh or dried, instant sheets.
Spinach and ricotta tortellini small rounds of pasta, filled with spinach and ricotta, then sealed.

PAWPAW Tropical fruit also known as papaya.

PECANS Golden-brown, buttery, rich nuts. Good in savoury and sweet dishes.

PEPITAS Dried and hulled pumpkin seeds.

PIDE Turkish bread made from wheat flour; comes in long flat loaves and small rounds.

PINE NUTS Also known as pignoli; small, cream-coloured kernels from the cones of various pine trees.

PIZZA SAUCE We used a ready-made pizza sauce consisting of tomatoes, herbs and spices.

POCKET PITTA Lebanese wheat-flour bread that can be split to form a pocket.

POLENTA A flour-like cereal made of ground corn (maize); similar to cornmeal but coarser. Also the name of the dish made from it.

POTATOES
Kipfler potato small and finger-shaped with a nutty flavour; good baked.
Pink eye small with deep pink eyes; good steamed, boiled or baked.
Tiny (baby) new potatoes also known as baby potatoes

or chats; these can be any variety of potato, harvested when young enough to retain a waxy appearance and paper-thin skin.

PRAWNS Also known as shrimp.

PROSCIUTTO Salted-cured, air-dried (unsmoked), pressed ham; usually sold in paper-thin slices, ready to eat.

PUMPKIN Sometimes used interchangeably with the word squash, the pumpkin is a member of the gourd family. Various types can be substituted for one another.

RAISINS Sweet dried grapes.

REDCURRANT JELLY
A preserve made from redcurrants; used as a glaze for desserts and meats, or in sauces.

kumara

baby new potato

pink eye potato

kipfler potato

RICE
Arborio small, round-grain rice; especially suitable for risottos.
Brown natural whole grain.
Calrose a medium-grain, extremely versatile variety.
Paper mostly from Vietnam (banh trang). Made from rice paste and stamped into rounds. Dipped momentarily in water, they become pliable wrappers for fried food and fresh (uncooked) vegetables.
Puffed grains puffed under heat.
Wild from North America, but not a member of the rice family. It is expensive as it is difficult to cultivate; has a distinctive flavour.

ROCKMELON Also known as cantaloupe.

ROLLED OATS, TRADITIONAL Whole oat grains that have been steamed and flattened. Not the quick-cook variety.

ROSEWATER EXTRACT Made from crushed rose petals; used for its aromatic quality in many desserts.

SAMBAL OELEK Also ulek or olek. A salty paste of ground chillies, sugar and spices.

SAUCES
Barbecue tomato-based sauce used to marinate and baste.
Black bean made from fermented soy beans, water and wheat flour.
Fish also called nam pla or nuoc nam; made from salted, pulverised, fermented fish. Has a pungent smell and strong taste; use sparingly.

Hoisin a thick, sweet and spicy Chinese paste made from salted, fermented soy beans, onions and garlic; used as a marinade or baste, or to accent stir-fries and barbecued or roasted foods.
Oyster Asian in origin, this rich, brown sauce is made from oysters and their brine, cooked with salt and soy sauce; thickened with starch.
Plum a thick, sweet and sour sauce made from plums, vinegar, sugar, chillies and spices.
Soy made from fermented soy beans.
Sweet chilli a comparatively mild, Thai-type sauce made

from red chillies, sugar, garlic and vinegar.

Tabasco brand name of an extremely fiery sauce made from vinegar, hot red peppers and salt.

Teriyaki a sauce consisting of soy sauce, corn syrup, vinegar, ginger and other spices; a distinctive glaze on grilled meats.

Tomato also known as ketchup or catsup; made from tomatoes, vinegar and spices.

Worcestershire a dark-brown spicy sauce used to season meat, gravies and cocktails, and as a condiment.

SESAME SEEDS Black and white are the most common varieties of these oval seeds. To toast: spread seeds evenly on oven tray, toast in moderate oven briefly.

SNOW PEAS Also called mange tout ("eat all").

SOURDOUGH Crunchy, crusted bread with soft inner crumb, a distinctive aroma and a sour flavour.

SPINACH (ENGLISH) Delicate, green leaves on thin stems; good eaten raw or steamed. The vegetable often called spinach is correctly known as Swiss chard, silverbeet or seakale.

STAR ANISE A dried star-shaped pod, the seeds of which taste of aniseed.

STOCK 1 cup (250ml) stock is the equivalent of 1 cup (250ml) water plus 1 crumbled stock cube or 1 teaspoon stock powder.

SUGAR We used coarse, granulated table sugar, also known as crystal sugar, unless otherwise specified.
Brown an extremely soft, fine granulated sugar retaining molasses for its deep colour and flavour.
Caster also known as superfine or finely granulated table sugar.
Icing sugar mixture also known as confectioners' sugar or powdered sugar; granulated sugar crushed together with a small amount (about 3%) of cornflour added.

Palm sugar from the coconut palm; usually sold in compressed cakes. Also known as gula jawa, gula melaka and jaggery. Brown sugar can be substituted.
Raw natural brown granulated sugar.

SUGAR SNAP PEAS Small pods with formed peas inside; eaten whole, raw or cooked.

SULTANAS Golden raisins.

TACO SEASONING A packaged seasoning made from oregano, cumin, chillies and other spices.

TANDOORI PASTE Indian blend of spices, including turmeric, paprika, chilli powder, saffron, cardamom and garam masala.

TAT SOI Also known as rosette pak choy, tai gu choy, Chinese flat cabbage; a variety of bok choy.

TEMPEH Flat cakes made from soy beans. Tofu may be used instead.

TIKKA MASALA Indian paste of chilli, coriander, cumin, garlic, ginger, turmeric, oil, fennel, pepper, cinnamon and cardamom.

TOFU Also known as bean curd; off-white, custard-like product made from the "milk" of crushed soy beans; comes fresh, as soft or firm, and processed, as fried or pressed dried sheets. Fresh tofu can be refrigerated in water (changed daily) up to 4 days.

TOMATOES
Egg tomatoes also called plum or Roma; smallish, oval-shaped tomatoes.
Paste triple-concentrated tomato puree used to flavour soups, stews and sauces.
Puree canned pureed tomatoes (not tomato paste). Substitute with fresh peeled and pureed tomatoes.

TORTILLA Round, unleavened bread, made from either corn (maizemeal) or wheat flour.

VANILLA BEAN Dried, long, thin pod from an orchid. The minuscule black seeds inside the bean are used to impart a luscious vanilla flavour in baking and desserts.

VINEGAR
Balsamic vinegar authentic only from Italian province of Modena; made from a local wine of white Trebbiano grapes specially processed then aged in antique wooden casks to give the exquisite pungent flavour.
Brown malt vinegar made from fermented malt barley and beech shavings.
Cider vinegar made from fermented apples.
Raspberry vinegar made from fresh raspberries steeped in a white wine vinegar.

Red wine vinegar based on red wine.
Rice vinegar made from fermented rice. Also known as Seasoned Rice Vinegar.
Sherry vinegar mellow wine vinegar named for its colour.
White wine vinegar made from fermented white wine.

WATER CHESTNUTS Resemble chestnuts in appearance, hence the English name. Small brown tubers with a crisp, white nutty-tasting flesh. Their crunchy texture is best experienced fresh, however canned and frozen water chestnuts are more easily obtained and can be kept about a month, once opened, under refrigeration.

WATERCRESS Small, crisp, deep green, rounded leaves having a slightly bitter, peppery flavour. Good in salads, soups and as an ingredient in sandwiches.

WONTON WRAPPERS, FRESH Small raw pastry wrappers. Gow gee, egg or spring roll pastry sheets can be substituted.

YELLOW BABY SQUASH Also known as pattypan, summer squash or scallopine. Yellow or green thin-skinned squash.

ZUCCHINI Also known as courgette.

sourdough

bagel

lavash

pide

ciabatta

pitta pocket

INDEX

MAKE YOUR OWN STOCK

These recipes can be made up to 4 days
ahead and stored, covered, in the
refrigerator. Be sure to remove any fat
from the surface after the cooled stock
has been refrigerated overnight. If the
stock is to be kept longer, it is best to
freeze it in smaller quantities.

Stock is also available in cans or tetra
packs. Stock cubes or powder can be used.
As a guide, 1 teaspoon of stock powder or
1 small crumbled stock cube mixed with
1 cup (250ml) water will give a fairly
strong stock. Be aware of the salt and fat
content of stock cubes and powders and
prepared stocks.

All stock recipes make about 2.5 litres (10 cups).

BEEF STOCK
2kg meaty beef bones
2 medium (300g) onions
2 sticks celery, chopped
2 medium (250g) carrots, chopped
3 bay leaves
2 teaspoons black peppercorns
5 litres (20 cups) water
3 litres (12 cups) water, extra

Place bones and unpeeled chopped onions
in baking dish. Bake in hot oven about
1 hour or until bones and onions are well
browned. Transfer bones and onions to
large pan, add celery, carrots, bay leaves,
peppercorns and water, simmer,
uncovered, 3 hours. Add extra water,
simmer, uncovered, further 1 hour; strain.

CHICKEN STOCK
2kg chicken bones
2 medium (300g) onions, chopped
2 sticks celery, chopped
2 medium (250g) carrots, chopped
3 bay leaves
2 teaspoons black peppercorns
5 litres (20 cups) water

Combine all ingredients in large pan,
simmer, uncovered, 2 hours; strain.

FISH STOCK
1.5kg fish bones
3 litres (12 cups) water
1 medium (150g) onion, chopped
2 sticks celery, chopped
2 bay leaves
1 teaspoon black peppercorns

Combine all ingredients in large pan,
simmer, uncovered, 20 minutes; strain.

VEGETABLE STOCK
2 large (360g) carrots, chopped
2 large (360g) parsnips, chopped
4 medium (600g) onions, chopped
12 sticks celery, chopped
4 bay leaves
2 teaspoons black peppercorns
6 litres (24 cups) water

Combine all ingredients in large pan,
simmer, uncovered, 1¹/2 hours; strain.

facts and figures

Wherever you live, you'll be able to use our recipes with the help of these easy-to-follow conversions. While these conversions are approximate only, the difference between an exact and the approximate conversion of various liquid and dry measures is but minimal and will not affect your cooking results.

dry measures

metric	imperial
15g	$\frac{1}{2}$oz
30g	1oz
60g	2oz
90g	3oz
125g	4oz ($\frac{1}{4}$lb)
155g	5oz
185g	6oz
220g	7oz
250g	8oz ($\frac{1}{2}$lb)
280g	9oz
315g	10oz
345g	11oz
375g	12oz ($\frac{3}{4}$lb)
410g	13oz
440g	14oz
470g	15oz
500g	16oz (1lb)
750g	24oz ($1\frac{1}{2}$lb)
1kg	32oz (2lb)

liquid measures

metric	imperial
30ml	1 fluid oz
60ml	2 fluid oz
100ml	3 fluid oz
125ml	4 fluid oz
150ml	5 fluid oz ($\frac{1}{4}$ pint/1 gill)
190ml	6 fluid oz
250ml	8 fluid oz
300ml	10 fluid oz ($\frac{1}{2}$ pint)
500ml	16 fluid oz
600ml	20 fluid oz (1 pint)
1000ml (1 litre)	$1\frac{3}{4}$ pints

helpful measures

metric	imperial
3mm	$\frac{1}{8}$in
6mm	$\frac{1}{4}$in
1cm	$\frac{1}{2}$in
2cm	$\frac{3}{4}$in
2.5cm	1in
5cm	2in
6cm	$2\frac{1}{2}$in
8cm	3in
10cm	4in
13cm	5in
15cm	6in
18cm	7in
20cm	8in
23cm	9in
25cm	10in
28cm	11in
30cm	12in (1ft)

measuring equipment

The difference between one country's measuring cups and another's is, at most, within a 2 or 3 teaspoon variance. (For the record, 1 Australian metric measuring cup holds approximately 250ml.) The most accurate way of measuring dry ingredients is to weigh them. When measuring liquids, use a clear glass or plastic jug with the metric markings. (One Australian metric tablespoon holds 20ml; one Australian metric teaspoon holds 5ml.)

If you would like to purchase *The Australian Women's Weekly* Test Kitchen's metric measuring cups and spoons (as approved by Standards Australia), turn to page 120 for details and order coupon. You will receive:

- a graduated set of 4 cups for measuring dry ingredients, with sizes marked on the cups.
- a graduated set of 4 spoons for measuring dry and liquid ingredients, with amounts marked on the spoons.

Note: North America, NZ and the UK use 15ml tablespoons. All cup and spoon measurements are level.

We use large eggs having an average weight of 60g.

oven temperatures

These oven temperatures are only a guide. Always check the manufacturer's manual.

	°C (Celsius)	°F (Fahrenheit)	Gas Mark
Very slow	120	250	1
Slow	150	300	2
Moderately slow	160	325	3
Moderate	180 - 190	350 - 375	4
Moderately hot	200 - 210	400 - 425	5
Hot	220 - 230	450 - 475	6
Very hot	240 - 250	500 - 525	7

how to measure

When using graduated metric measuring cups, shake dry ingredients loosely into the appropriate cup. Do not tap the cup on a bench or tightly pack the ingredients unless directed to do so. Level top of measuring cups and measuring spoons with a knife. When measuring liquids, place a clear glass or plastic jug with metric markings on a flat surface to check accuracy at eye level.

Looking after your interest...

Keep your Home Library cookbooks clean, tidy and within easy reach with slipcovers designed
to hold up to 12 books. *Plus* you can follow our recipes perfectly with a set of accurate
measuring cups and spoons, as used by *The Australian Women's Weekly* Test Kitchen.

TO ORDER

Mail or fax Photocopy or complete the coupon below and post
to AWW Home Library Reader Offer, ACP Direct, PO Box 7036,
Sydney NSW 1028, *or* fax to (02) 9267 4363.

Credit cards Have your details ready then, if you live in Sydney,
phone 9260 0000; if you live elsewhere in Australia,
phone 1800 252 515 (free call, Mon-Fri, 8.30am-5.30pm).

PRICE

Book Holder Australia:
pre-GST $11.95, post-GST $13.15
(GST takes effect July 1, 2000).
Elsewhere: $A21.95.

Metric Measuring Set Australia:
pre-GST $5.95, post-GST $6.55
(GST takes effect July 1, 2000).
New Zealand: $A8.00.
Elsewhere: $A9.95.
Prices include postage,
handling and GST.
This offer is available
in all countries.

PAYMENT

Australian residents We accept the credit cards listed on the coupon, money orders and cheques.

Overseas residents We accept the credit cards listed on the coupon, drafts in $A drawn on an
Australian bank, and also British, New Zealand and U.S. cheques in the currency of the country
of issue. Credit card charges are at the exchange rate current at the time of payment.
